Two Speed World

T0347171

| Hh | Harriman House

Harriman House is one of the UK's leading independent publishers of financial and business books. Our catalogue covers personal finance, stock market investing and trading, current affairs, business and economics. For more details go to: www.harriman-house.com

Two Speed World

The impact of explosive and gradual change – its effect on you
and everything else

Gerald Ashley & Terry Lloyd

HARRIMAN HOUSE LTD
3A Penns Road
Petersfield
Hampshire
GU32 2EW
GREAT BRITAIN

Tel: +44 (0)1730 233870
Fax: +44 (0)1730 233880
Email: enquiries@harriman-house.com
Website: www.harriman-house.com

First published in Great Britain in 2010
Copyright © Harriman House 2010

The right of Gerald Ashley and Terry Lloyd to be identified as Authors has been asserted
in accordance with the Copyright, Design and Patents Act 1988.

ISBN: 978-1-906659-70-7

British Library Cataloguing in Publication Data
A CIP catalogue record for this book can be obtained from the British Library.

Printed and bound in Great Britain by CPI Antony Rowe, Chippenham.

To my wife, Cynthia
and my sons, Ian, Philip and Michael
TL

To Karen
GA

Contents

About the authors

Gerald Ashley is an advisor, writer and speaker on business risk and decision making. He has over thirty years experience in international finance, having worked for Baring Brothers in London and Hong Kong, and the Bank for International Settlements in Basel, Switzerland. He is now Managing Director of St. Mawgan & Co which he co-founded in 2001, a London-based consultancy specialising in strategy consulting, risk management and decision making in finance, business and risk-taking. He is a Visiting Fellow at Newcastle Business School and a regular contributor in the press.

Terry Lloyd has spent over thirty years in the world of business development. Trained as a mechanical engineer, he joined Rolls Royce Aero Engines in the compressor design office, before joining the Mechanical Engineering Department of Nottingham University, within a team solving technical problems using early computer systems. During his time there he was awarded his PhD. He then moved into mainstream computing where, at Perkin Elmer, he helped to design and develop the first commercial software suite for mini-computers. From there he moved into financial software including trading room technology and financial data. He is now a director of St. Mawgan & Co.

www.twospeedworld.com

Preface

Change alone is eternal, perpetual, immortal.

Arthur Schopenhauer (1788-1860)

What will happen next? What is just around the corner? What if some people could see just that bit further ahead, and better still before anyone else? Imagine the enormous advantage it would give them to be always in front of the competition and able to gain an advantage over the next person, or rival, or deadly enemy.

Humans spend a great deal of time thinking about the future, sometimes trying to relate it to the past, sometimes considering their options and how their choices will affect what is to come. This ability to conjure up thoughts, desires, hopes and fears about the future has been a key element in evolutionary development – the aptitude to create abstract thought has led to enormous advances by humankind.

This ability enables people to hold and recall memories of past events in their minds, which they can then link into an endless number of sequences, discarding the majority while retaining as stories those sequences that they judge to be important and significant. The recall of past events, weaving them into explanatory stories and storing them for future recall, is conducted when people are doing little else – they are daydreaming.

Framing the past in this way is the only way that people can cope with new situations; evaluating alternative plans and executing them in a timely fashion as soon as they recognise a situation that matches one of their stories. If there is no match then they are *at a loss* for what to do. Future events that are dealt with in this way can run from the trivial to life changing, from life threatening to golden opportunities – people are in a constant battle to make sense of the perceived future, sometimes to shape it, but always trying to put themselves in a position to cope with change.

In this book we have two primary aims: firstly to examine the nature of change and secondly to consider what are the best tools and strategies to cope with, exploit and possibly instigate change.

In tackling our first aim – to examine the nature of change – we define the two types of change as incremental (low speed) and disruptive (high speed). Change can always be assigned one of these categories and so everyone lives in this two speed world. It is an important distinction because how change should be tackled depends on which type of change is in play. Change is not fixed within one of the two types – it can migrate from one mode to the other, perhaps starting as a disruptive change and reducing to a slower speed. For instance, one can easily imagine a disruptive change, a sudden earthquake or a breakthrough technological advance such as the harnessing of electricity, that has a major impact at first but in time becomes less disruptive and only has incremental effects going forward. This is particularly true in the field of invention where the breakthrough usually leads to a long tail of small but still important incremental changes. Furthermore, one man's incremental change can be another man's disruption. A business disruption in one firm, its bankruptcy say, may only lead to an incremental increase in business for another firm.

> **❝** In tackling our first aim – to examine the nature of change – we define the two types of change as incremental (low speed) and disruptive (high speed). **❞**

Our second objective is to introduce different decision-making tools that are available and describe where each is applicable. This ensures that people are aware of the range that is available to them and avoid choosing an approach which could make a difficult situation worse. We highlight the fact that many decision makers tend to see most issues in incremental terms and that on occasions, for example during a financial crisis, they fail to understand that there is disruptive change underway that demands different analyses and approaches to those that they employ in normal times.

We explain what drives change and what equips people to deal with the future by using stories from the past. We will find that although circumstances may differ the basic characteristics of change do not. It is only necessary to look back over the past 150 years – a very small sample size indeed of human life on earth – to see how changes such as technical innovations, war and social upheavals affected the lives of earlier generations. There is every reason to expect that the world of the future will see similar upheavals, or greater ones.

Telling this story provides the opportunity to introduce a number of notable world changers from the past, who are almost without exception very colourful characters. We meet the devisor of a tool that gives an overall perspective of any large-scale problem. He was also an astronomer who had an assistant fire a gun in the direction that his telescope was pointing in an unsuccessful attempt to reduce turbulence. We also meet an American engineer who ended up being awarded Japan's Second Order Medal of the Sacred Treasure; a futurologist on whom the film character Dr Strangelove was partly based; a serial inventor who started life as a stuntman and water escapologist; and another who attempted to sell Neville Chamberlain a Death Ray system which he claimed could kill an army of 1,000,000 in one go.

This book tells a straightforward story, but it is drawn from a large array of sources and its creation has only been possible as a result of one of the most important disruptive changes of recent years, namely the inception of the internet. This has enabled us to cover the extremely wide range of human knowledge that the subject matter requires, read the histories of manmade and natural changes, and examine the tools that are available to manage changing circumstances. Without the aid of the internet we should have needed to spend longer in the British Library than Karl Marx to research this book. We have necessarily omitted many interesting side roads and so where appropriate we have provided a reading list in a references section at the end of the book so that readers can investigate particular topics in greater detail.

Finally, we would both like to particularly thank John Perry, David Bieri and Percy Coats for their thoughts, ideas and observations, and we should like to thank everyone at Harriman House for their help and encouragement.

Gerald Ashley & Terry Lloyd

London, November 2010

1

From Here To Uncertainty

He that will not apply new remedies must expect new evils: for time is the great innovator.

Francis Bacon (1561-1626)

Everyone's future will involve change, whether dramatic or mundane, but what is the nature of change? Are there in fact different types of change, and can differing techniques be applied to cope with it, to manipulate it and hopefully take advantage of it?

What at first sight may be a simple matter of trying to estimate the future and its impact turns out to be a much more subtle subject. Many factors quickly come to mind. Is change sudden or a slow creeping process? Is the impact of change dramatic, or a steady incremental movement? Do any changes truly occur in isolation, or is the world in fact in a form of continuum where – to borrow Niles Eldredge and Steven Jay Gould's idea about natural evolution – things tick along steadily and then are punctuated by a sudden shift in events and outcomes? To address these questions change must be considered from many different angles, including its nature and its defining characteristics.

This chapter sets the scene, explaining the difficulty of looking forward *at all* given the unimaginable complexity of the world and the tendency of people to behave irrationally in the face of such uncertainty. The general issue of human rationality, particularly when encountering unexpected change, appears in many guises, but provided that such behavioural pitfalls are recognised and avoided, then with appropriate simplifications there is a way to prepare for the future.

Surprisingly the principal simplification, that of dividing future events into those arising from incremental change and those arising from disruptive change, is mirrored within the brain – which deals with events in two distinct ways, either step-by-step, or by non-linear thinking. This metaphor is valuable, since it stresses the necessity of both modes of thinking to ensure complete comprehension of the world in which the brain must function. Furthermore, people cannot control the future unless they can handle both varieties of change.

One Inch Forward Lies Darkness

In order to understand the future it must be simplified. The first step in any simplification process is to assume that events are independent of each other. Consider a few random events such as the rising of the sun in the morning, the winning of the British Open golf tournament and rain falling at some time on a given day. Crucially, by keeping these events separate, the human brain can more easily understand them. However, it must always be borne in mind that through its interconnections, the real world is much more complicated than an imagined collection of unrelated events.

A very simple example is that if a particular golfer's playing style favours dry conditions, then his performance in the British Open will depend on the weather during the tournament. Obvious, but it is an iron rule of analysis that all thinking, assumptions and decisions must be checked against the simplifications on which they are based, some of which may be hidden, seemingly unimportant or totally disconnected. In our case, we started out thinking the weather and the British Open were separate events, but of course one does impact the other.

Having simplified the situation by reducing all events to independent occurrences, the next step is to consider the likelihood of every event occurring. This too can only be achieved with simplification. The sun rising in the morning is a practical certainty in our lifetimes *but* it is a practical impossibility in the astronomically long-term future when our sun will no longer exist, having exploded. Certain events such as death depend upon measurable factors such as annuity tables and gender, but there are many additional factors that are hard to evaluate, such as improvements to health care, or the occurrence of some catastrophe, or just a simple accident, which mean estimating the timing of this certain event is impossible.

As before, the rule here is not that these simplifications should not be made, but that it is important to always check for reasonableness of assumptions. When a Goldman Sachs executive famously said in 2008 (after very sharp financial market moves) that "we are seeing things that were 25-standard deviation moves, several days in a row," he was guilty of failing to keep checking. If the usual statistical assumptions held, then just one such move would be expected to occur only once in $6x10^{124}$ (that is 6 followed by 124 zeroes) lives of the universe. What actually happened was that the market conditions changed so much that they invalidated the assumptions on which his models were based.

Changing labels and changing plans

The Japanese proverb quoted at the start of the section – one inch forward lies darkness – suggests that the future is so difficult to predict that it is not worth trying. Perhaps this is too pessimistic, but it is a useful warning in a world where confident predictions of things to come are based on assumptions that are by no means assured. While many events are practically certain and others are practically impossible, a lot of the most important events are inconveniently situated between these extremes.

Whilst simplifying labels are important, providing a convenient shorthand and indicating how an event should be handled, they can be fluid. The label that is attached to an event may not be permanent, but changed by the occurrence of *other* events. A sudden earthquake, a volcano erupting, a declaration of war, a new invention, a change in legislation, or a host of other things, can force a relabelling. When this happens, plans should be changed as soon as it is practical to match the fresh circumstances, but this does not always happen since people resist changing plans that are already underway.

Once a plan has been agreed, there is a belief that changing it is a sign of weakness. If its execution is already in train, then expenses will have been incurred that it may not be possible to retrieve, so inevitably people find it easier to convince themselves to plough on rather than admit defeat, conduct a re-evaluation and start again. Behavioural economists call this phenomenon the *sunk cost bias*, and it arises regularly in the field of decision making and risk taking. The British politician Denis Healey coined the phrase "When in a hole stop digging!" This is sound guidance that cautions against falling foul of the sunk cost bias, but it is often very difficult advice to follow.

Coping with complexity

When looking at change in the round it can be seen that a large number of diffuse factors create a complex set of inputs that affect people's ability to forecast future events. Is the change likely to be sudden or incremental? Is it a measurable risk or a complete unknown? Is it an isolated event, or dependent on the resolution of other events?

In spite of this complexity, much of human decision making seems to be instinctive and, despite a lack of rationality on occasions, it is a measure of humankind's success that it is still on the planet and, in general, prospering. However, humans do on many occasions get it wrong, and an understanding of the mechanisms involved in estimations of the future and the decision-making process would certainly be valuable.

Understanding in many areas of decision making and risk has certainly progressed significantly in the last 100 years or so. Alongside this, research and experience have suggested many ways to improve our performance in the face of uncertainty and thereby secure better outcomes. In the later chapters some of these advances will be described and their use by government, industry and individuals will be explained. These techniques include improved gathering and interpretation of qualitative information and more sophisticated analysis of quantitative data.

Even so, in spite of these advances, because the whole idea of planning and coping with future change is a complex web of interdependencies, biases and judgements, there can be no perfect answer. Whilst it is attractive to look for a silver bullet, in many situations that is impossible and it is prudent to attempt to be ready for any eventuality. By definition, the future, and the change that will come with it, is fluid and often incomplete.

Perhaps that one inch forward is pretty murky after all.

Certainty, Risk, Uncertainty And Impossibility

In 1921 the American economist Frank Knight wrote *Risk, Uncertainty and Profit*, in which he sought to simplify the task of looking into the future. Essentially Knight divided information into four categories, as can be seen in Table 1.1.

Table 1.1 – Frank Knight's four types of information

Certainties	These include known historical and verifiable facts – dates of Presidential elections in the USA for example.
Risks	Events that are known with a good degree of probability. This is where there are good levels of data that can be modelled to arrive at reasonable predictions based on probability (usually employing the bell curve), for example mortality tables, where from past data estimates of life expectancy can be extrapolated.
Uncertainties	Events where there is too little data to properly model it in terms of probability. This is often where predictive models suffer from mission creep, when in the desire to create risks with fairly predictable boundaries models are applied where there is insufficient data. This is also known as Knightian Uncertainty. For example, trying to predict terrorist events, when the data available is too small to give any meaningful indications for the future.
Impossibilities	Events that are unrepeatable or illogical, for example repeating the events of a previous day, or water flowing uphill.

Knight's work provides an interesting sidelight on understanding change and trying to predict the future. Generally *certainties* and *risks* imply incremental extrapolation from the present with an emphasis on routine and detail, while *uncertainties* and *impossibilities* imply a lack of historical data and disruptive, or explosive, changes. This categorisation clearly shows the fundamental difference between the two types of future development and why they must be handled differently. It is all too easy to always use techniques that are good for incremental change, since that is the norm and is what general procedures are set up to handle. However, these techniques will do more harm than good if they continue to be used in the face of disruptive change.

Routine And Detail

The basic human desire is for certainty, even if it is the certainty of impossibility, and change is often avoided when it brings risk or uncertainty. We see this in such aphorisms as: 'At least you know where you are', 'If it ain't broke don't fix it' and 'If it was good enough for my father then it is good enough for me'.

For most people, if change is unavoidable, then quantified risk is preferred over total uncertainty. In a study by researchers at Cambridge University in 2008 it was demonstrated that financial traders were more stressed by uncertainty than by the prospect of failure. This desire to anchor the mind onto definite outcomes and focus on solutions which offer precise results may seem at variance to the observation that humans are curious creatures who are very adaptive and able to think in an abstract manner. This contradiction is explained by considering priorities. Our first priority is to survive and this is best achieved through certainty, but when survival is assured our curiosity takes over and then, and only then, do we seek out the new.

The comfort of facts and the threat of disruption

In a world where certainty is much prized, it is not surprising that many people are engaged in securing this comforting state of affairs. The work of many professionals such as accountants, actuaries, town planners and civil servants is concerned with gathering facts and ordering them so that plans can be instigated, and the progress of these plans monitored against a known risk. In the Conan Doyle story *The Copper Beeches* our hero Sherlock Holmes admonishes Watson for airily pontificating on possible clues: "Bring me facts Watson, I need facts, I cannot build bricks without clay," the detective cries. Holmes' plea for facts is the natural first step all people take when trying to make sense of things, whether in the past, present or future. Indeed C.P. Scott, the celebrated editor of the *Guardian* newspaper, went further saying "Comment is free, but facts are sacred".

A large part of any worldview is based on facts, whether simple observations, considered deductions, or carefully worked out rules and laws that can be considered immutable. Facts are the concrete base on which risks are quantified and from there strategies, projections and predictions are built with safety. For example, the fields of science and medicine are built upon such an evidence-based approach. Perhaps it is natural to consider facts as sacred.

An important element in this is to simplify evidence to the point that it and its implications can be understood. The most powerful tool for simplifying data is the statistical concept of the normal distribution, or in popular parlance the bell curve (how this is done is explained in Chapter 5). If it is treated with respect, a normal distribution of past facts can provide an elegant tool for understanding all sorts of problems. In the financial world, it can be used to predict the smoothing effect of holding a portfolio of shares rather than shares in a single company. It can be used to predict the increased volatility that results from gearing investments and it can be deployed to measure how an active fund manager is performing against a passive portfolio. The sheer power of the normal distribution brings dangers, as there is a temptation to use it when the underlying assumptions no longer hold true. It was failure to check the underlying assumptions of the bell curve that tripped up the Goldman Sachs executive referred to earlier.

On top of quantitative facts, the importance of qualitative facts must not be underestimated and indeed in earlier times the latter were much more important than the former. An important mechanism for passing on such facts, particularly before the advent of general literacy, was through storytelling. This is a key human skill, which equips people for the future by passing on experience from the past.

So words, numbers and even pictures are gathered, stored and subsequently employed – through the *soft* technique of storytelling and the *hard* route of mathematics – to prepare for the future.

* * *

Everything that has been considered so far assumes that the future is based upon what has happened in the past. This is the boring and plodding world of incremental change – life in the comfort zone, where a dull advance over a long period of time can add up to a great deal of progress. Exceptional events, such as wars and new inventions, disturb this equilibrium and consequently are etched on people's memories. This natural tendency is reinforced by the media, which concentrates on new and eye-catching events in order to sell its wares.

These amplifiers mean that disruptive changes receive more attention than their importance warrants, relative to the incremental changes of everyday life. As a result, people are more likely to make donations to a charity for a sudden catastrophe such as a flood, rather than to one concerned with ever-present poor sanitation. The behaviour behind this false reasoning is called *vividness bias* and it arises directly from the two distinct ways that incremental and disruptive changes are perceived.

The two speed world is just one mechanism by which people are confused and led to behave in irrational ways, for there is a large body of research in the field of behavioural science which confirms that people often fool themselves. People may like to fondly believe that they are rational agents, able to weigh and assess facts dispassionately and without bias, but the truth is somewhat more complicated. The human mind constantly frames and anchors facts, as well as opinions, speculations and downright wishful thinking, in a number of biased ways.

Then The Explosion

It is a truism that not everything in life runs along in a nice steady manner. Everyone experiences situations where there is a sudden, even explosive, change in circumstances. The effects of such disruptive events can range from the irritating to the awesome. Natural disasters provide some of the most vivid examples. In 1600 more than two million people died in Russia from a famine caused by the eruption of a volcano in Peru. Not only was this particular event far reaching geographically, but its impact echoed through decades because tragically the economy of Peru took some 150 years to recover to its pre-eruption levels.

Here two important consequences of disruptive change are on display: it is impossible to predict its scale and impact, and its consequences can reverberate for many years or decades, or longer. Terrorist events, sudden shifts in technology and changes in legislation can all create a huge disturbance to the status quo and render irrelevant the settled facts that were analysed in static models.

It is therefore patently difficult to react to a situation when the causes are a mixture of vivid, disruptive events and expected events. Should money be spent on flood defences, or road safety? Should more attention be paid to rioters, or to letters to newspapers? When faced with this all too common mixing of events, the *vividness bias* can come to the fore. This is confirmed by research which has shown that when estimating the causes of a death, people underestimate highly likely causes such as heart disease, stroke and cancer, and overestimate more vivid causes such as food poisoning, electrocution and even dying in a tornado.

In the two speed world, it is very difficult to keep a proper weighting in our judgements, or more precisely humans are not often completely risk sensitive – biases keep barging into the judgement process. People seem overwhelmingly drawn to the drama of a sudden change, or to an outcome that has more vividness attached to it, and as a result often falsely give too much prominence or weighting to it.

All change please

The components of a manmade disruptive explosion can be illustrated by the explosive growth of railways in Britain. Here are all the elements of a huge and irreversible disruption in transport, communication and engineering.

In the early nineteenth century, Liverpool was an important port and Manchester, some 30 miles away, a growing industrial city. To join these important cities, a new company was set up to build a railway between them. In 1829, the newly created Liverpool and Manchester Railway was almost complete, but the means of propulsion was still to be decided from the alternatives of steam locomotives, horses and stationary winding engines. The company's directors decided to evaluate the practicality of using steam engines by running trials on part of the newly completed track at Rainhill. The trials were held in a carnival atmosphere with between 12,000 and 15,000 people watching from specially erected grandstands. As everyone now knows, the winner was Stephenson's Rocket, which completed the trials at an average speed of 12mph.

Within a year the service was operating and although its main aim had been to convey freight between the docks and the factories, the great surprise turned out to be passenger traffic. Perhaps as a result of the razzamatazz of the Rainhill Trials, in the first year of working the railway carried nearly half a million passengers who paid over £100,000 in fares, against an initial estimate of just £10,000. This stunning early success highlights the truth about disruptive change in business – that the outcomes, whether good or bad, can never be accurately predicted. This is not surprising since there are often no precedents on which to base meaningful, let alone accurate, predictions.

The immediate result from the successful locomotive trials and the subsequent successful passenger service was that many other people saw an opportunity to make money and triggered what became known as the Railway Mania. This peaked in 1846, when no less than 272 special Acts of Parliament were passed on behalf of railway schemes. The initial disruption sparked by Stephenson's Rocket was felt for an enormously long time and around the globe; steam engines continued to be built in Britain until 1960 and the railways continue to this day, even using that original track. What is striking is that a single event, the building of the railway, swamped everything else around it, as previously stable businesses were threatened and the old tried and tested methods could not meet the new challenges.

Probably the most badly affected by the sudden success of the railways were the canals and the stagecoach network. The first canal in Britain, the Bridgewater Canal named after the Duke of Bridgewater, had been completed in 1776 to link coal mines to their important market in Manchester. This in itself was a disruptive change, halving the price of coal in the city and initiating Canal Mania. The resultant network of canals was principally used to carry heavy freight, because barges only travelled at walking pace. Needless to say they were hard hit by the railways with their massive increase in speed and pulling power and by the 1850s the cargo carried by canals had shrunk by two-thirds. Meanwhile passengers who had been using mail coach to travel between major cities from the 1780s quickly deserted to rail as it offered much greater speeds than the 10mph offered by the coach service.

One of the greatest positive impacts of the development of railways was the opportunity that they gave people to live outside of the cities which provided their employment. Commuter towns were even developed by railway companies to create demand for their lines; the 1920s pioneer of this form of development being the Metropolitan Railway in London. This initiative encouraged many to move out of central and inner-city London to suburbs such as Harrow and further out to commuter villages in Buckinghamshire and Hertfordshire.

An endless list of disruptive changes

The coming of the railways was just one of many disruptive changes that have transformed the world. Powered ships now bring cheap imports, challenging and in many cases destroying local and less efficient farming and industry. The motorcar, which is arguably one of the great disruptors of the twentieth century, has an immense thirst for oil and this in turn has given enormous wealth and political power to previously impoverished countries in the Middle East that can provide the black gold. More recently the digital camera that is built into mobile phones has turned everyone into newspaper photographers and signalled the near death of photographic film.

The list of human created disruptors is almost endless, and a common theme is that the people who triggered the changes had no idea of the full implications and consequences of what they started. The disruptive environment is a journey without maps and so the full outcomes are pretty well impossible to see at the start.

History generally remembers the success stories but to add a word of caution, there are many forgotten failures for every remembered success. The erasing of failures and lauding of triumphs is called the *survivorship bias* and this is yet another behavioural prism through which events tend to be distorted. Invention is by its nature a matter of hit or miss,

> **The disruptive environment is a journey without maps and so the full outcomes are pretty well impossible to see at the start.**

and usually it is miss. Later in this book we investigate the personality types that are drawn to invention and it is no surprise that they must be prepared to ignore the scorn of others, try the unlikely and above all persevere. For now though, let's look further at the human brain and how it is biologically set up to deal with different types of activities and different types of change.

Two Brains Are Better Than One

Crucial to dealing with incremental and disruptive change is the requirement for very different modes of thinking. Let's consider why this is.

To manage incremental change one needs skill in written language, logical deduction, categorisation and the ability to perform actions sequentially, while to manage disruptive change one needs skills at understanding metaphors, non-linear thinking, the capacity to resolve incongruity and a sense of the big picture. In fact the brain *does* deal with events in these two distinct fashions and so it is natural to suspect that different parts of the brain are involved in controlling such very different thought processes.

This idea is reinforced by the fact that physically the brain consists of two almost completely separate hemispheres and naturally one feels that this complication must have a purpose. The plausible conclusion is that everyone effectively has two brains in their head, one for dealing with each type of problem. It is known that speech is strongly connected with areas on the left side of the brain, so it is tempting to broaden this observation to other activities and conclude that different sides of the brain are working in different ways.

In reality this is an over simplification since both hemispheres of the brain seem to be involved in almost everything. Nevertheless there are some very striking differences in the methods used by the two hemispheres. The left hemisphere tends to deal more with bits of information in isolation, matching the nature of tasks associated with incremental problems, while the right hemisphere deals with entities as a whole, matching the needs of a disruptive problem for which there are no standard rules for solution. The management guru Robert Heller says "The left side [of the brain] has an irritating devotion to numbers, analysis, logic, etc, concerning itself with cash flow and the dire consequences of mismanagement of finances. The right side deals with more romantic ideas and imagination rules."

Split-brain research

Interest in this topic grew largely from split-brain research in the 1960s, that later won Roger Sperry of Caltech a Nobel Prize. In the 1940s, one treatment for epilepsy was to sever the corpus callosum, the thick bundle of nerve fibres that forms the main communications path between the two sides of the brain. This gave Sperry the raw materials for his investigations (which are unlikely to be repeated, as epilepsy treatment today is mainly through drugs). From his studies of these people, he concluded that "everything we have seen indicates that the surgery has left these people with two separate minds. That is, two separate spheres of consciousness". He also said that "there appear to be two modes of thinking, verbal and nonverbal, represented rather separately in left and right hemispheres respectively".

Subsequent attempts to refine these early results have been largely inconclusive, as every identifiable human activity seems to be served at some level by both hemispheres. More recent research based on brain scanning using magnetic resonance imaging, which was not available in the 1960s, was conducted by clinical neurologists Fink and Marshall. Their work is still in progress and to date the results are confused. They have so far established that it is still reasonable to associate global processing with the right side and attention to detail with the left side of the brain even though the issue is not clear-cut, and it is really a case of a grey scale rather than black and white. Current research by neuroscientists is now putting more emphasis on how the two sides of our brain complement and combine with one another.

The left/right brain metaphor

Whatever actually goes on inside a person's head, there are clearly different versions of the world that are delivered and with two minds acting separately in this way, it is not surprising that a person exhibits the biases that were introduced earlier. One version emphasises logical deduction and one emphasises non-linear gut feeling. It is a useful metaphor to associate the former with the left hemisphere and the latter with the right hemisphere, as long as it is remembered that this is a metaphor and not necessarily connected to which neurons fire to solve a particular problem. On this basis the left-brain/right-brain paradigm can be matched with the detail/big picture capabilities that are needed to handle, respectively, incremental and disruptive changes.

The school system reflects the left-brain/right-brain paradigm with specific training addressing the left-brain needs and general education the right-brain needs. An example of specific training is preparing for qualifications in the professions, where uniformity across all practitioners is vital. Some educationalists complain that a results-focussed schools system concentrates on such left-brain training, and as a consequence right-brain general education is neglected. It is perhaps no accident that the success or otherwise of right-brain education is difficult to calibrate in a manner that satisfies today's target-obsessed culture.

Human resources departments in the commercial world use two sets of tests to grade candidates, which reflect this division. One set tests aptitude and ability, which measures left-brain skills, while the second set evaluates personality and interests, addressing the right-brain skills. This is discussed further in Chapter 3. Schooling and subsequent employer testing creates a very two-dimensional world where apparently its inhabitants are suited either for dealing with incremental changes or with disruptive changes, but not both. In the real world many people are somewhere in the middle, although most have a general inclination to be either a left-brainer or a right-brainer.

Cultural divide

The Snow dichotomy

In 1959, C. P. Snow, a physicist, civil servant and successful novelist wrote an essay entitled 'The Two Cultures and the Scientific Revolution'. This predates Roger Sperry's work and so there is no direct reference to left-brain and right-brain, but Snow does describe the problem in terms of two cultures – the sciences and the humanities – which matches the left-brain/right-brain metaphor. Snow's complaint was that most people live exclusively in one camp or the other.

In the essay, Snow highlighted the often wilful lack of communication between scientists and literary intellectuals. He argued that formal training, where students were segregated according to their natural strengths, magnified their inherently different mindsets to produce a nearly complete lack of understanding and communication across these two cultures. This he regarded as a major hindrance to solving the world's problems. If he were alive today, he would no doubt regard the inability of many journalists to grasp

> **"** Most people regard themselves as a right-brainer or a left-brainer when what is often required is people who can switch between the two as the need arises. **"**

modern scientific problems such as global warming as depressingly predictable, and feel that nothing has progressed. Snow's principal point was that most people regard themselves as a right-brainer or a left-brainer when what is often required is people who can switch between the two as the need arises.

A recent illustration of the Snow dichotomy has arisen in the world of finance where there is concern about insufficient communication between the financial engineers who devise complex instruments (overwhelmingly left-brainers) and the traditional senior management (who tend to be right-brainers).

Quantitative pricing and statistical risk measures are black arts to most senior managers, who must therefore accept figures from the financial engineers without question. Meanwhile senior managers must also wrestle with broader issues of economics, politics and human behaviour. It is clear that for a financial institution to be efficient and effective it should be run by people capable of both types of reasoning and the two groups must understand each other's viewpoints and the basis for their analysis. A simple but effective management rule should be that all decisions must be taken using judgements that are based both upon experience and the relevant empirical evidence.

The danger of left-brain supremacy

Some people believe that not only are there two tribes here, but that the wrong tribe is winning. Iain McGilchrist, in his book *The Master and his Emissary*, argues that, despite its inferior grasp of reality, the left-brain is increasingly taking precedence in the world, with potentially disastrous consequences. He uses the parable of a Nietzsche story in which a wise master, using right-brain skills to see the whole worldview or *Gestalt*, trained his emissaries, brought up in the left-brain approach of treating individual information in isolation. The cleverest and most ambitious vizier began to see himself as superior and became contemptuous of his master, who was usurped and eventually the domain collapsed in ruins. McGilchrist believes that this story illustrates a number of problems in the Western world, where the domination of the left-brainers, who should by rights be servants, threatens civilisation.

This left-brain antagonism is not without evidence. It does seem that the more numerous left-brainers have historically tended to be suspicious of the illogical right-brainers. Before the twentieth century the internal wiring of the brain was not known or understood but interestingly the conflict in thinking styles was recognised and reflected in language. Good things have tended to be associated with the right hand (left brain) and the left hand (right brain) was linked to bad events and outcomes. (Somewhat confusingly, the right side of the brain controls the left side of the body.) For example the Latin word for left is *sinister*, while in Latin the word for right is *dexter*, hence dexterity. In French left is *gauche*, hence gawky, while the French for right is *droit*, hence adroit.

It is a team game

In spite of the relic in language of right-handedness (left-brain thinking) being positive and left-handedness (right-brain thinking) being negative, there is no right or wrong in these two modes of thinking. McGilchrist's conclusions are bold but at the very least it seems that a balanced approach is needed. Whilst plenty of left-brainers are required to implement plans and strategies they should not be allowed to crowd out the smaller but vital number who are right-brain dominant in their thinking. Left-brain thinking has many appeals, but if uncontrolled it can stifle innovation and creative thinking.

What is of crucial importance is to understand that the different approaches can only be successfully employed in the appropriate situations. This goes to the heart of understanding change and working through to the future. Certain issues or problems are weighted towards left-brain thinking and others towards the right. It is too dogmatic to say an issue is purely right or left side, but if the wrong emphasis is applied then there is a danger of making the outcome worse and not better.

It is a modern management mantra to entreat everyone to think out of the box (right-brain thinking), when in fact what is probably needed is for most of them to stay in the box (left-brain thinking) and not hijack any area that is not within their range of understanding and control.

Today Disruption Is Everywhere

Free capital is the key

The speed of change is connected to the amount of free capital that there is in the world to drive it. Capital in this sense is not just money but it is also time and creative resources. If people do something new, from building Stonehenge to digging the Channel Tunnel, then they must be fed and supported during the construction period. Even the clichéd solitary inventor in the garden shed needs time and maybe some spare income in order to develop his or her

> **"** It is a modern management mantra to entreat everyone to think out of the box (right-brain thinking). **""**

ideas. Alternatively the speed of change can be raised by borrowing in times of emergency such as war, so almost inevitably new things appear during a time of prosperity or enforced spending. In peacetime, anyone who only just has enough money to keep body and soul together is unlikely to have spare time and resources to devote to experimental ideas that may lead to future advances, but which have a high chance of failure.

The last two centuries have been a time of increasing prosperity for the Western world and consequently new products and services have been raining down at an ever-increasing rate. Many of these developments have a multiplier effect, particularly those related to communication, such as the train, the motorcar, the airliner, radio and television, and the internet. These developments that are now taken for granted have turned a collection of city states and a myriad of subsistence communities into a single interconnected world – an increasingly global village. It is the powerful combination of prosperity and interconnection that has laid down the landscape that guarantees that the world will continue to throw up new things.

Every new thing needs detail added in order to turn it into a practical solution. It is this tricky bridge from disruptive discovery to incremental development where so many ideas fail. The motorcar needed reasonable roads and a comprehensive fuel distribution system before it became a practical reality. The internet needed personal computers and useful content before it became ubiquitous. This bridging is somewhat like the links between right-brain thinking and left-brain thinking – ways to link the two together are needed to bring about success. Critically every successful conversion from brainwave to practicality needs an understanding of the significance of the new idea, whatever it is, and the ability to build a project capable of realising its potential. This involves planning of time and money, promotion, and creating an organisation to build and sell the product, or service. This important topic is considered in Chapter 6.

Increasing specialisation

The world has responded to this overall acceleration by increasing specialisation. From the early development of the division of labour, through to just-in-time delivery of parts and services, there have been massive advances in this process. This may explain why left-brainers have become so important during the industrialisation of the world, but as previously emphasised it would be wrong to let them control everything. The professions who control the implementation of new ideas have seen more and more specialisation, and as a result continue to subdivide and proliferate. A London recruitment consultancy warns potential students that there are nine possible paths to a career in accountancy (AAT, ACCA, ACT, CF, CFE, CIMA, CIPFA, ICEAW, JIEB/CPI) and they should look at their long-term aims before embarking on any one of them. Generally the certificates that they earn demonstrate the left-brain skills of their holders, but as the world fragments, it indicates an ability to tick more and more boxes within an ever smaller form.

With this huge number of new initiatives, most of which contain a high degree of complexity that are beyond the scope of the individual mavericks of old, it is important to keep an overall perspective. Sometimes the people charged with delivering the new initiatives do not achieve this, particularly if they are divided into two teams who are broadly antagonistic towards each other.

The objective in this book is to enable the reader to understand the importance of balance – to stop left-brainers from applying inappropriate analysis and equally to stop right-brainers from jumping from one bright idea to another in an unstructured fashion and as a result achieving nothing.

In Summary

Change is affecting our lives continuously, both with imperceptible and incremental advances and with buffeting from large disruptive events. Although there may be events which contain both incremental and disruptive changes, the effects can be more easily understood by separating these two classes since they are both perceived and handled differently which explains some observed behavioural biases. Precedence for making such a separation is provided by the human brain, where logical tasks are handled quite differently from those involving intuition. Both incremental and disruptive events have been affecting the human race throughout history and it is convenient to examine changes through examples from the past, the effects of which are fully developed.

Broadly speaking, incremental changes are embedded into the daily routine and facilitate survival. In earlier times they consisted of finding food and shelter and of evading the attention of predators, while today they consist of the tasks necessary to earn a living and maintain a home. Positive disruptive changes are what enable the human race to progress, through new inventions, new knowledge and new alliances. Each class of change must be approached in the way that is suitable to its needs. This is particularly important at the present time as an ever increasing number of disruptive changes vie with the established incremental world for finite resources. The human race must survive and wants to

" Broadly speaking, incremental changes are embedded into the daily routine and facilitate survival. Positive disruptive changes are what enable the human race to progress, through new inventions, new knowledge and new alliances. "

progress, so both types of change are important, but to start with, in the next chapter, we look at the world of incremental change.

Dead Reckoning

2

Not everything that can be counted counts,
And not everything that counts can be counted

Attributed to Albert Einstein (1879-1955)

A t any one time, the majority of people are doing what they have done on many occasions before. Routine – and the incremental change it brings – is the norm. Whilst people may strive for more excitement and variety, in practice most of their lives and experiences tend to be within a narrow compass. There are good reasons for this: there is comfort in routine, although everyone rails against it; there is efficiency in slow incremental change and steady working patterns; and those who are established in the upper strata of society, business and government often have little incentive to incite more disruptive change.

Within the structure of routine and steady environments there are two main anchors: mental activities, which are guided by memories and written records; and physical activities, which are achieved and perfected by learned skills. These processes provide the Established Practice through which individuals, groups and institutions create tried and tested techniques that deliver efficient results.

The fact of routine and experience delivering efficient results can easily be observed. Some 20 years ago a BBC television game show called *The Generation Game* revolved around the idea of two teams attempting to emulate a simple everyday task after a demonstration from an experienced operator. The entertainment came from seeing the glorious ineptitude of the contestants when for the first time they attempted to lay bricks, throw a clay pot, or make a hospital bed. The adage *practice makes perfect* was never so well illustrated. In its own way the programme demonstrated just how many skills are required for certain professionals to be able to carry out their everyday tasks efficiently and competently.

As explained in Chapter 1, the world is running at two speeds, with sudden bursts of change from time to time disrupting the steady jogging pace of incremental changes. Incremental change is the result of the pursuit of *Established Practice*. This is not a completely static process, but it is fundamentally slow and broadly predictable. Since it follows naturally from the past, incremental change can be understood by measuring what went before. In such a world, making measurements and predictions makes perfect sense; when to plant seeds, when to harvest crops; when to fish, when to stay in harbour. This is a world of broad stability where knowledge-based rules of thumb or more technical heuristics work well. There can still be cyclical effects, but these often reinforce the feeling of stability and still lend themselves to a degree of predictability.

This chapter explains how Established Practice is at the heart of everyday life. Rules and reliable measurements that support those rules enable the state and big business to control large populations through routine and order. Furthermore, knowledge can be codified into rules and hidden from others to give a competitive advantage. Focussed training ensures that everyone can follow the rules, while repetition brings maximum efficiency and productivity. With these

> **"** Incremental change is the result of the pursuit of Established Practice. **"**

advantages, those in authority are naturally against radical change, but so too are the governed, because it would render their narrow skills useless and upset their reassuringly stable environment. Overall Established Practice has provided crucial factors in the fight for survival of the human race, but this chapter also shows that their very popularity presents the danger that they might be followed blindly, even when they should not be.

Little By Little

Routine leads to efficiency through predictability, but it is also an important framework through which command and control are maintained. Those in authority are fond of Established Practice, since these practices help ensure that they retain power. Royalty, landowners, the church, and more recently governments and monopolistic industries, defend the status quo when it suits them to do so, even though on occasions they rely on very convoluted arguments. Here the seventeenth century Catholic Church is wrestling with the disruptive notions of Galileo:

> For to say that, assuming the earth moves and the sun stands still, all the appearances are saved better than with eccentrics and epicycles, is to speak well; there is no danger in this, and it is sufficient for mathematicians. But to want to affirm that the sun really is fixed in the centre of the heavens and only revolves around itself (i.e., turns upon its axis) without travelling from east to west and that the earth is situated in the third sphere and revolves with great speed around the sun, is a very dangerous thing.

Equally in the world of commerce there are strong motives for maintaining the status quo. Firstly, this is because it is almost certainly of economic benefit to do so, since any variation from Established Practice is likely to incur extra costs, at least in the short term. Secondly, as practitioners in current methods are established in existing businesses, they would lose their special advantage over new entrants if new ideas replaced the old. This means that Established Practice is frequently turned into a difficult barrier for any newcomers to surmount. As described earlier, the development of canals in England by the wealthy aristocratic landowners of the day was a big investment and unsurprisingly they vigorously opposed the development of the railways because this new technology was rightly viewed as a threat to their investment.

Some may argue that the commercial world is more flexible than that, and that progress through innovation is an important driver, but this depends on the business. The more established and dominant a business, the less need for a progressive attitude. Why take the risk of wasting time and money? Of course, by contrast, new ventures in uncertain territory with unpredictable futures are strongly motivated to try new things. Until their path to success and a settled future is in place, it makes sense to keep an open mind and challenge the existing environment. This attitude is epitomised by the upstart computer software companies of the 1970s and 1980s, who over time have settled into a comfortable middle age, centred around defending their bountiful patch rather than venturing forth.

Interestingly there is a strong body of research that suggests that humans dislike too much choice, often feel paralysed by it and so prefer a relatively narrow and routine decision landscape. Many workers feel more comfortable if they have a routine. Despite protestations about wanting to be different and to avoid boring work many people are happy with routine – not deadbeat monotony but a degree of routine around which they can anchor their daily lives.

Frequently workers in a specific industry or practice have skills which give them an edge over outsiders, but which may have no application in a changed world, so unsurprisingly the status quo is fiercely defended by these people. This attitude may also be informed by the business cycle – at tough times workers are far less willing to risk job hopping, while in more prosperous times workforces are more mobile, as a leap into something new is deemed less risky when a retreat to the existing field remains available. Such attitudes can also percolate through personal lives where a degree of routine is helpful if it cuts down the number of choices and avoids wasting time and money.

Show Me The Money

An essential tool for any authority to maintain its grip is the ability to measure the output of its workers against the output of previous years. This ranges from simple organisations of a few people and processes, through large organisations and industry, right up to running and governing a country. In extreme cases of autocracy, measurement can be taken to extraordinary lengths, as in the Soviet Union where an entire Ministry of Economic Planning set prices for *everything*. Even in more democratic set ups, governments need sophisticated command and control mechanisms that are predicated on accurate and timely measurement. Whether it is raising taxation, defending the state, sponsoring strategic industries, or encouraging new science and technology, measurement is at the core. So across all organisations a culture and formal structure of Established Practice is central to managing things.

It should not be surprising then that throughout the development of civilisations, the ability to measure accurately has been a much prized and sought after skill. From accurate weights and measures in the Middle Ages, to chronometers for navigation, to lasers for huge distances, and electron microscopes for minute distances, the advance of measurement has been breathtaking. Across almost all fields of human endeavour there have been enormous advances in evidence gathering, which is then used to inform what is to be done next.

Measuring to manage

The Domesday Book was one of the first serious exercises in nationwide measurement undertaken in the Western world since the Roman Empire. Having successfully seized the English throne, William the Conqueror needed to know how to distribute the tax burden that had to be applied in order to pay for the defence of England from possible invasion from Scandinavia, and to pay for costly battles in northern France. To obtain the necessary information he commissioned a comprehensive land survey to assess the extent of the land and resources in England at the time. Although the information was collected in the space of around a year, William died before he could use it for its intended purpose. However, as an unintended consequence, in the Domesday Book he has left us with an incomparable snapshot of life in the eleventh century.

William's son, Henry I, ascended the throne in 1100 and continued the process of refining measurements in order to ensure the flow of taxes into the royal coffers. To do this he introduced a new monetary system known as the tally stick, which effectively took the control of issuing money from private goldsmiths and gave it to the Crown. The tally stick was marked with a system of notches and then split length-wise as a simple way to prevent counterfeiting. The two halves both had the same notches and each party to the transaction received one half of the marked stick as proof, thereby providing a means to record bilateral exchange and debts. Henry required that royal taxes be paid with tally sticks rather than by coin. This in turn encouraged their use amongst the citizens of Medieval England and amazingly the practice survived until 1826. As with the Domesday Book there was an unintended consequence when, in 1834, the redundant tallies were burned in a stove in the Houses of Parliament. Unfortunately the fire got out of control, setting the building on fire and razing it to the ground.

Throughout the Renaissance period, taxation by the ruler continued to be the principal reason that regular accounts were needed. Businesses themselves only created rudimentary accounts when some event, such as the death of the owner or a partner, necessitated it. In medieval times annual accounts were unheard of and would have been thought very strange and unnecessary. The only exception to this rule was when the authorities tried to levy a specific tax, meaning that proof of ownership and a business valuation was needed.

So, although the Italian academic Luca Pacioli is credited with inventing double entry accounting in the fifteenth century and we are encouraged to see him as the father of accounting, his methods were hardly in use. However, with the emergence of business taxation and the growth in trade and related finance, more sophistication slowly developed. Annual accounting valuations gradually became the norm, and received a further boost when business owners and investors started to demand that their money work harder and so needed a more accurate view of their financial status. For example, by the 1880s American steel tycoon Andrew Carnegie was receiving daily cost sheets detailing each and every single expenditure at his steel works.

Command and control

This trend towards recording, monitoring and managing has continued ever since, with the early twentieth century seeing the development of time and motion studies, the increasing use of corporate taxation, the reporting requirements of stock exchanges, etc. In manufacturing, the development of just-in-time delivery and all the supporting logistics is a triumph of ever more refined and improved measurement and management.

In banking and finance in particular there has been a growing demand for evermore complex and detailed reporting. The ability to value positions and manage assets has grown hugely as markets have developed and the financial services and products that are offered have rapidly expanded. The demands on measurement systems have been commensurately huge, because staff that can move huge sums around by a simple keystroke need to be closely controlled and monitored. This means that modern finance is a web of instruments, systems and processes which are interconnected in complex ways. All of these measurement regimes are central to managing all these people and processes and all have contributed to a large body of Established Practice in finance, most of which is closely regulated.

In organisations or groups in a settled environment that believe they have a precise knowledge of the facts, and believe that their systems and processes have been honed by Established Practice, there can arise a culture where if anything goes wrong, then there must always be a guilty party to blame. Naturally this can lead to a defensive culture and one that is fearful of innovation and new ideas. Armed with statistics and audit trails, managers are often able to pinpoint failures and apportion blame from their evidence. In the pure world of measure and manage, sales people lose bonuses or their jobs for not making their numbers, while managers are demoted or dismissed for not managing time or budgets according to plan. All of this assumes a very predictable environment with no sudden shocks or surprises, however the problem is not always the fault of the person penalised, but in fact may be caused by some external shock to the system. It might be that a new competitor has come into the market and made the target unreachable for the sales person; the price of raw materials may have shot up, invalidating the budget predictions, etc.

> **There can arise a culture where if anything goes wrong, then there must always be a guilty party to blame.**

The desire to manage away all risk

This thinking can extend beyond the business world so that even in everyday life any unanticipated event is considered to be an avoidable accident which must be placed at someone's door. This attitude has grown a great deal in recent years, perhaps as a by-product of more and more sophisticated measurement tools. Such thinking can lead to an extreme attitude of risk aversion and an unwillingness to take any risks, however small. The thinking runs like this: if someone falls over, then it should have been foreseen and since it was not, someone is to blame.

Such a culture of risk aversion leads to unbelievable precautions taken by government authorities and other bodies. Prompted by such overzealous thinking, in two years 68 English local councils spent more than £1.65 million on certified German-built *topple-testers* designed to apply a predetermined amount of force to suspect gravestones to see if they would wobble. This was all in order to find out whether or not the stones could bear the weight of an average-sized teenager. This is a perfect example of over-measurement posing as prudent management.

AJP Taylor said, "Until August 1914 a sensible law-abiding Englishman could pass through life and hardly notice the existence of the state," but as life becomes more complex through car ownership, foreign travel, home ownership, the Welfare State, etc., interaction between state and citizen is greatly increased. The government intervenes in more and more aspects of life and in order to do so, demands more and more facts and figures, but unfortunately not always the right figures. The bursting of a global credit bubble in 2007 was a massive disruptive change but the knee-jerk reaction was for regulation that was suited to command and control, and to plump for further ways to reinforce Established Practice.

At the onset of the credit crunch many observers were quick to criticise the existing regulatory framework, and accused it of being too laissez faire with an inappropriate light touch typical of Anglo-Saxon finance. Well how light? The FSA Rule Book is more than 8000 pages in length! Interestingly the handbook, which is being constantly revised and updated, grows inexorably with every new edition. Over 2000 pages alone were added in 2007 when new rules covering equity trading were introduced and a (comparatively small) additional 497 pages were written up in January 2008 as the first response to the credit crunch.

Some regulatory experts have sought to claim that this modest expansion of rules actually underlines the FSA's commitment to principles-based regulation, and demonstrates that it has not moved towards a prescriptive regime. This seems very myopic, for the fact is that incremental institutions, such as the FSA, are only really able to control incremental changes, since they have nothing in their decision making DNA that enables them to understand or address disruptive changes. Their stock response to any change, incremental or disruptive, is to load up on more Established Practice.

Knowledge Truly Is Power

So Established Practice is a central tool of command and control, particularly when running a nation state. One of government's primary needs is for information in order to be able to run a controllable state and oversee a stable and effective economy. If, in addition, the state is the unique possessor of commercial information which gives them an edge over their trading competitors and perhaps rivals and enemies, then so much the better. The age-old saw that knowledge is power was fully understood from the earliest of times.

In the Middle Ages, before the availability of legal protection of commercial and intellectual property, ruling authorities, mainly monarchs and barons rather than formal governments, acted as central monopolies and did everything in their power to control and conceal any valuable know-how or special advantage. The obvious solution was to institute Established Practice, where the small number of people with the know-how could be controlled and monitored. This is a double-edged sword, since while it preserves existing knowledge, at least until the inevitable leak, it provides an environment that is hostile to any further advances. State monopolies, through their restrictions, deter those who would attempt breakthroughs and new ideas, and as a result they tend not to happen in these circumstances.

Silk, glass and medicine

The monopolistic power of the state is well illustrated by the Chinese silk industry. For some 3000 years until around 300AD China carefully guarded the skills developed in the making of silk and a culture of top-down incremental control was rigidly enforced. The silk workers' techniques and processes were closely guarded secrets and the penalty for revealing them or smuggling the vital silkworm eggs or cocoons outside of China was death. As international trade developed, it inevitably became harder for the state to control these secrets and in time the Chinese lost their monopoly on silk production. The production secrets leaked west to India and ultimately throughout the Roman Empire. Bad news for the former monopoly holders in China, but good news for overall global trade and prosperity.

Similarly, skilled glass working started in the Middle East and entered Europe through its main trade gateway, the dominant trading port of Venice. The Venetian authorities recognised what a valuable skill they had acquired and from 1291, their local guilds guarded their knowledge fiercely. Just like the Chinese, the Venetian authorities threatened death to anyone who betrayed the valuable commercial secrets. To control the industry, the government strictly regulated both the incentives and the conditions of the workers and the trading terms of the various firms and employers, but despite their best efforts enough expertise escaped to allow rival enterprises to start elsewhere.

However, it was a disruptive change in the form of a new technique which eventually caused the downfall of the Venetian glass industry. Antonio Neri, a Florentine priest and chemist, defied the authorities and published a comprehensive description of glass-making techniques. His book, *L'Arte Vetraria* (*The Art of Glass*) was translated into English in 1662 and it explained how better glass could be made by replacing the potash used at that time with lead. This was quickly taken up by the English businessman George Ravenscroft who produced the first clear lead crystal glassware on an industrial scale. By 1800, British lead crystal had overtaken lime-potash glasses on the continent, and England replaced Venice as the centre of the glass industry. Neri's book had explained how to make glass economically and, cut loose from monopolistic controls, the resultant industry rapidly expanded and developed a huge range of new products thus turning glass into a utilitarian substance affordable to all. Venice's loss was the world's gain.

One final example of the wresting of secrets from a monopolistic organisation comes also from mid-seventeenth century England.

London-based apothecary Nicholas Culpeper challenged the strict controls laid down by the main medical authority of the day, the College of Physicians. Having married well, Culpeper used his wife's money to set up a pharmacy in Spitalfields, deliberately just outside the control of the rigid City of London authorities. In an age when medical books were only written in Latin, Culpeper wrote a number of important works in English. Suddenly a much wider audience could read about medical matters, drugs and medicines and were able to heal themselves rather than have to find money to pay the large bills of physicians and apothecaries.

* * *

All of the above lessons demonstrate the unwanted side of Established Practice, which by its nature seeks to control and maintain certain processes and procedures, and in so doing stifles fresh thinking and innovation. By protecting vital information, the Chinese silk industry and the Venetian glass makers ruled their respective markets for hundreds of years and this secrecy provided huge rewards for their holders. However, the wider marketplace suffered – who knows how long the introduction of glazed windows was delayed by the secrecy of Venice?

Most aspects of life are routine and lend themselves to regimentation, but if the control that is applied is total, then further beneficial breakthroughs are prevented and progress stalls.

Training And Education

The mind is not a vessel that needs filling, but wood that needs igniting.

With the above comment the Greek philosopher Plutarch (46-127AD) encapsulated the difference between training and education. A trainer fills students' minds with facts and figures as someone might pour water into vessels. An educator shows students how to work things out for themselves as someone might light a piece of wood that thereafter carries on burning. We will now think about which of these approaches has value in our world today.

The tradesman's apprentice

Training is ideally suited to facilitate Established Practice, as the trainer possesses all of the necessary knowledge to ensure its continuance. Today it is mainly associated with the principal professions, such as law, accountancy and medicine, where a combination of examinations and on the job training leads, on successful completion, to a certificate that assures the public of a

> **“** Training is ideally suited to facilitate Established Practice, as the trainer possesses all of the necessary knowledge to ensure its continuance. **”**

satisfactory level of competence. Historically training was exemplified by the master craftsman and his apprentice and since the skills that were required to be a mason, blacksmith, wheelwright or butcher changed little from one generation to the next, the apprenticeship was the ideal training scheme for both the employer and the employed. The employers could ensure that the scheme was focussed on the needs of the business and nothing more and that when they employed someone with the apprenticeship qualification they knew that the person would be able to do the job. At the same time, in a stable and predictable jobs market the employee qualified in this way knew that there would always be work available.

In the United Kingdom the tradition of apprenticeships goes back many years – as long ago as the twelfth century young boys were put into the care of a guild's master craftsman to learn a lifelong trade. Parents would be expected to pay a premium to the craftsman and the young lad would be bound by an agreement for up to seven years. In 1563 this was first codified in English law by the Statute of Artificers and Apprentices, which regulated and protected the apprenticeship system. Other legislation followed and right up until after the Second World War the apprenticeship system was a vital part of training in British industry.

More recently, the traditional apprenticeship has come under threat as the continuity from one generation to the next has broken down and many traditional trades have either disappeared or been completely transformed by new technologies. The statistics tell the story, with the numbers in apprenticeships falling from 240,000 in the mid-1960s to 53,000 in 1990. They have now rebounded back up to 180,000, but only after the creation of the Modern Apprenticeships structure in 1994. The challenge of creating a system that satisfies today's needs from one that originated in the old world is indicated by the fact that this new structure needs 180 distinct apprenticeship frameworks to cover today's specialities and it is inevitable that these frameworks will need regular modifications and additions going forward.

Training that is suitable for a fast-changing environment is a worldwide problem that different governments have tackled in different ways. Germany has remained broadly traditional and there is a much heavier emphasis on apprenticeships for skilled positions, with correspondingly fewer university graduates compared to other Western countries. In order to achieve this,

Germany has a very wide variety of apprenticeships to cover all requisite areas and certification is provided for over 400 separate occupations.

Interestingly the United States provides a direct contrast with Germany and does not generally provide targeted training. Its high schools educate students of all abilities and interests in one learning community and a single standard must be achieved by all students in order to receive a uniform diploma. However, there is a movement towards vocational education and unions such as electricians, ironworkers, sheet metal workers, plasterers and bricklayers now offer apprenticeships, as do some trade associations. Both in China and Japan apprenticeships and a strong adherence to Established Practice are the norm.

The need for flexible education

In addition to the problem of trying to match standardised training to a changing world, there is the further danger that the smaller, but vital, group of future *game changers* are being overlooked. Criticisms have been raised in England and France to the effect that the public education system is letting these key people down. Peter Hyman, a teacher, complains that the British government attitude is "we'll spoon-feed you the required information to pass your exams". Maëlle Lenoir of the Association Paris Montagne says: "The French system of learning is founded on a strict learning of knowledge, rather than on creativity or innovation". Both are concerned that the education systems in their respective countries are limited to producing people who can fit comfortably into the existing world.

In such a system, children have a rigid framework from the early years right through until they graduate from university – education (actually *training*, in terms of the definitions laid out above) becomes a form of conveyor belt that manages students' progress and keeps them within limits. Professional training or on-the-job apprenticeships can follow this pattern too, which continues the process of fitting the student and employee into a standard template. This is ideal for the world of Established Practice – the world of incremental change – but is quite unsuitable for the creative types that we shall meet in Chapter 3.

Perhaps there is a single solution to both problems. As will be shown in Chapter 5, the only way to prepare for situations which do not have a probable outcome is to be ready for anything. If it is not possible to identify the training that is necessary for lifetime employment, then a general flexible education that can be adapted to changing conditions as they arise is required. Coincidentally this is just what game changers need, since their educators cannot foresee what direction they will ultimately take. In Plutarch's words *filled vessels* are needed to promote and maintain Established Practice, but this must be complemented by *ignited wood* to handle unpredictable challenges that arise.

Repetition, Repetition, Repetition

Another facet of Established Practice that is illustrated by the history of Venice is the development of organised routines into industrialised mass production.

The key to the prosperity of the great city state was the trade between the Middle East and Europe. Indeed, as we saw earlier, it was such trade that had brought the glass making secrets to Venice. Trade depended upon sailing ships and crucially upon shipbuilding capacity – which was satisfied by Venice's extensive and sophisticated shipyards. Shipbuilding had begun in Venice as far back as 1104 and by the time the industry reached its peak in the early sixteenth century it was employing some 16,000 workers, making it the world's largest industrial base prior to the Industrial Revolution. Routines developed over the centuries meant that Established Practice in the yards had reached the highest level of sophistication possible at the time.

It was here that a mass production system was devised with standardised parts in which the newly built ships were towed up to ten at a time past the windows of storehouses where stores and equipment were added. By the time the ships reached the end of the dock, an early production line, they were ready to sail. It became a source of Venetian pride to show important visitors their whole process; starting with a keel in the morning and having a complete and fully seaworthy vessel by evening. On one particularly notable occasion in 1574, for the benefit of Henry III of France, the whole operation was completed while some 3000 guests were banqueting.

Such standardised shipbuilding practices were echoed in the Second World War by the Liberty ships that were built in the United States to replace war-time losses. Building these cargo ships to a common design ensured fantastic productivity, whereby 18 shipyards built 2751 ships in five years. The ships were constructed from prefabricated sections that were welded together in assembly-line fashion. Initially, each ship took around 230 days to build, but the average eventually dropped to a remarkable 42 days, with the fastest recorded time four days and 15.5 hours from laying the keel to launch. As well as fast construction, the overall production levels were spectacular with three new Liberty ships being completed every day. By cutting out frills and variety aesthetics were sacrificed, but at a time of crisis routine and repetition delivered what was needed.

More than 400 years and 4000 miles separate these two shipbuilding stories, but the conclusion is the same. In manufacturing, when Established Practice is taken to the limit, almost unbelievable rates of construction are the result.

Dull Money

Established Practice has a long history in finance and any study of money and markets soon reveals many cycles and situations that endlessly repeat themselves. This suggests that adherence to tried and true methods is entirely sensible and pragmatic.

In finance, the idea is to generate efficiency gains through creating flexible but easy to replicate financial services. At its simplest level the basic requirement for a successful financial product, as far as the provider is concerned, is an adequate history of similar transactions and an environment in which the past conditions continue smoothly into the future. Life insurance, car insurance, credit card services, shares and bonds are markets which have spawned such standard financial products, each possessing the simplicity and efficiency that comes with development over a large number of years involving a large number of clients.

To help the assessment process, mathematical models are used to crunch historical data in order to value a business, judge capital requirements and price customer services, leaving in their wake an alphabet soup of acronyms and technical terminology. NPV (Net Present Value), VaR (Value at Risk) and ROA (Real Options Analysis) are just a few flavours from that soup.

In general the principles of such analysis are simple, but the complications that arise from market conventions, contractual agreements, taxation, cross dependencies and many other factors mean that the devil is most definitely in the detail. For interest rate calculations, even the number of days in the month depends upon the market concerned. These superficial complications make it difficult for the lay person to understand what is going on, but for the professional most calculations simply concern the extrapolation of past prices, subject to assumptions of the normal distribution, sometimes with modifications if experience shows consistent deviation from normal.

Buying and selling intangibles

Things started to get difficult for Established Practice in finance in the 1970s. The unchanging and almost rhythmic world of money experienced a disruption, which many thought was just an ordinary incremental change in the shape of formulae that enabled more accurate and crucially quicker calculation of derivative prices. In finance, a derivative is something which is bought and sold although it has no physical existence, but depends upon an underlying entity that does. This opened up huge new financial opportunities and products, which, allied with faster local computing power, unleashed a revolution. Many in the industry thought the old rules could be used for this new landscape, but they were wrong.

Pricing derivatives is probably one of the clearest examples of using historical data and mathematical algorithms. Some of these derivative instruments can be very complicated – not profoundly complex, but exceedingly detailed – while others are more straightforward. A simple derivative is an *option*, which in the financial world is the right to buy or sell at an agreed time, or during an agreed period, a specified amount of something (a commodity or equity for example), at an agreed price. Buying an option insures the purchaser against the underlying thing rising (by buying a *call*), or falling (by buying a *put*). The price paid for the option depends on all of the factors mentioned in the definition (buy/sell, expiry date or agreed period, current price of underlying, agreed price of underlying) plus one further factor, the volatility. This is the point at which price history enters the picture, for the volatility is based upon the normal distribution (which was introduced in Chapter 1) and more specifically standard deviation (which will be explained in Chapter 5).

Unfortunately the formulae used in the markets makes the rash assumption that there is always a fully liquid market, that is to say there is always someone to buy what another wants to sell, or to sell what another wants to buy. When this is true Established

Practice is fine and it is perfectly possible to model the past and price the future in the certain knowledge the market will always function. But as many events since the 1970s have shown, in times of panic markets melt away and past liquidity assumptions can look foolish, not to mention ruinous.

Keep Away From The Edge

The building of Venetian galleys and Liberty ships showed the benefits of following a pattern and using experience in order to streamline production. Similarly, standardised financial instruments can be built, provided that there is sufficient historical data and that data accurately models the present and future situations. This is the most efficient way to transfer risk around the markets, because standard terms and conditions ensure that all parties understand the implications of their actions. With these proven advantages there is always a temptation to push further and further away from the firm ground that is provided by a large historical database in a stable situation, towards the shakier ground that is provided by a market with fewer events, or a changing situation. Without realising it, people continue to apply Established Practice when the principles underpinning it no longer apply. This is a dangerous trap, for it can be folly to stretch measurement assumptions too far in the routine world. The path to hell is often paved with highly accurate and measured intentions.

" Without realising it, people continue to apply Established Practice when the principles underpinning it no longer apply. **"**

Model drift

For instance, Net Present Value (NPV) is a well understood accountancy concept for using the time value of money to appraise the value of long-term projects, but it depends on an assumed rate to discount future cash flows to their present values. If the chosen rate does not actually transpire, then the forecasts are wrong. Value at Risk (VaR) is a widely used measure of the market risk of a specific portfolio of financial assets, but if the assumed normal distributions do not apply and assets that are assumed to be independent are in fact correlated, then the measure is suspect and events that should have *once in a lifetime* probability will occur fairly regularly.

In corporate finance, Real Option Analysis (ROA) applies the concept of options to capital budget decision making. The options are typically used to measure the cost to make, abandon, expand, or shrink a capital investment. For example, the opportunity to invest in the expansion of a firm's factory, or alternatively to sell the factory, is a Real Option. These long-term methods often do not properly account for changes in risk over time and so present a false picture.

It is a very real concern when financial models are used inappropriately, for the Bank of England believes that this contributed to the credit crunch of 2007-2009. According to the Bank's Executive Director for Financial Stability, Andy Haldane, the failure of banks to count, manage and hedge their risks over a period of a decade was responsible both for the fantastic growth before 2007 and the crash that followed.

The meltdown in money markets that stemmed from the credit squeeze in 2007 was an event that banks' risk models indicated could happen only once in the lifetime of the universe, which as we showed in Chapter 1 simply indicates that the formula used in the risk models was invalid. In assessing reasons why the systems which banks use to gauge losses under worst-case scenarios could be so far out, Mr Haldane noted:

> Mathematical models were based on economic events in a very narrow window of time, as short as ten years. Bankers did not incorporate cross-correlations where the effect of adverse events in, say, the mortgage market, might trigger a move in others. Incentives were misaligned, so that when bankers maximised their individual rewards, it placed the bank in greater risk than was prudent.

Safe as houses

In general house mortgages represent an excellent way to satisfy both savers and borrowers, and usually can be considered an example of a steady if not static form of finance where any innovations are small and incremental. It should be the last place one would expect a massive disruptive change for the underlying principles are simplicity itself. People who need a house but who have no capital take out a mortgage; they are typically younger people with the time, energy and opportunity to earn money to service the loan. Meanwhile people with savings who need an income pay money into building societies or mortgage banks; they are typically older with few easy and safe opportunities to earn money, except through the income that their savings generate. This creates an Established Practice where experience has been built up over more than a hundred years and the underlying statistics are well known.

Unfortunately in the USA politicians who regarded home-ownership as part of the American dream pushed this steady market beyond its safe limits in the late 1990s by leaning on lenders to slacken their lending criteria. This invalidated the history on which the Established Practice was based, created a disruptive change par excellence and was arguably one of the principal causes of the credit crunch some ten years later. Here by pushing a stable system out of its steady incremental state a massive disruption was created.

Political pressure started in 1992 when US Congress enacted legislation which forced lenders to devote 30% of their lending to low and moderate-income borrowers. Pressure continued with the result that in 1994, the Mortgage Bankers Association eased its lending standards in order to increase lending to minorities and to immigrants. These political initiatives upset the established balance of lenders and borrowers and so additional deposits to fund the additional lending money had to be raised from further afield. This was achieved by selling securities or bonds with the underlying mortgage loans as collateral. The mortgage lender groups bundled together many loans and sold these grouped loans as securities called collateralised mortgage obligations (CMOs). Thus the funding gap between the existing deposit base and the newly expanded lending was filled. This looked like the perfect win-win situation – more borrowers were able to access the housing market, the lenders could expand their lending books and the government felt it was promoting a social good.

The hope was that the financial risk of the individual loans would be reduced by that aggregation process, but going back to Chapter 1, this assumes that the loans are independent and that what is going on in one low income household is unrelated to what is going on next door. In fact when things turn sour they often turn sour for everyone at once and this is the point that Established Practice breaks down. Once a few borrowers have defaulted, there are forced sales, the values of neighbouring properties fall and less money can be realised by the mortgage lender when there are further defaults. This caused a collapse of the housing market in 2008 and because the lenders had borrowed money from all financial markets, the contagion quickly spread through the financial world.

Peering over the edge

In 1972, in the early days of computer simulators, the Club of Rome commissioned what must be the ultimate example of pushing Established Practice beyond its limits, when they asked a team at MIT (Massachusetts Institute of Technology) to use the historical data for just five parameters (world population, industrialisation, pollution, food production and resource depletion) to predict future interactions between the earth and human systems. They went on to publish the results in a book entitled *The Limits to Growth*.

The headline conclusion of the report was that continued growth in the global economy without changes in behaviour, policy and technology would lead to planetary limits being exceeded sometime in the twenty-first century. Although the authors themselves explained the limitations of the analysis, the book caused a major stir at the time, with Yale economist Henry Wallich calling the work "a piece of irresponsible nonsense" while other critics falsely claimed that the book predicted that oil would run out in 1992.

A subject as important as the survival of the planet cannot be ignored simply because the prevailing technology is not ready for the task, but it will always be likely to attract fierce criticism, because the assumptions are easily challenged and there is much vested interest involved. As the MIT team demonstrated, trying to extrapolate from the state of the world today is going to be difficult even when there is only incremental progression. When we add in the inability of the models to foresee disruptions such as new oil finds, or OPEC crises, then controversy is guaranteed.

In Summary

Established Practice delivers consistent returns over a long period. It provides a knowledge base and measurement for rulers, governments and other authorities and it is this which gives them their power. With it, they can control a large population, reward the successful and punish any who fail to measure up to what is expected of them. Additionally, if the knowledge base can be hidden from the neighbours, then trading opportunities arise and the success is magnified.

Skills that support such practice emerged in the earliest days of human life and they have been crucial in ensuring the survival of the species. Hunting, fishing, building shelter and making clothes are all skills that have been transferred through thousands of years of history and to those early skills were added mental skills which enabled humans to learn from experience. People learned where the best fruit was to be found, where to plant grain and how to measure the seasons. Once writing became available, recording the harvest, noting transactions between tribes, families and individuals, all followed.

Established Practice incorporated all of this wisdom, in order to create the optimum way to live in the world. People recognised the value of this accumulated wisdom and so they revered the rules, advice and working practices that were handed down. This mindset continues to this day, even though the complexity of modern life invalidates some of the old certainties.

However, Established Practice alone is not enough, or all people of the world would still be living a hunter-gatherer existence and would be vulnerable to the natural disasters such as drought, floods and disease that regularly decimated the population in previous generations. These disasters continue, but their effects can be contained by modern aids such as airlifting food supplies, undertaking emergency civil engineering projects and by providing medical treatment. The human race has created these solutions by making occasional disruptive changes to the steady march of Established Practice, although the changes are often strenuously opposed by the authorities of the time and by the general populace who prefer the security of what goes under the heading of *tradition*. Training and the establishment of routine methods of working bring the maximum levels of efficiency, but at the same time they stifle innovations that could bring a step change. Furthermore, if the outside world alters, then attempts to continue without change can be fatal. The sorts of disruptive changes that upset the cosy world of Established Practice are described in the next chapter.

Disruptive Change

3

It is not the strongest of the species that survive, nor the most intelligent, but the one that is most adaptable to change.

Clarence Darrow, American lawyer (1857-1938)

We will now examine and consider disruptive change in detail. In this chapter we will look at why incremental models are not suited to disruptive change, the likelihood of failure as a barrier to creative thought, what sorts of people are creative and how they can be found, and what conditions generate speculative, novel thought for corporations and governments.

The critical thing to appreciate is that disruptive change cannot be understood as if it were an extreme case of incremental change. A precipice is not a very steep hill, an ocean is not a very large pond and a city is not a very large village. Simple benign experiences cannot be

> **" The critical thing to appreciate is that disruptive change cannot be understood as if it were an extreme case of incremental change. "**

extrapolated in order to understand an extreme event – it is so extreme that the existing incremental rules are no longer appropriate.

Going Over The Edge

A nice way to illustrate how incremental models can breakdown in seemingly routine circumstances is to look at data from stock markets. For example, a single day 5% drop in the NASDAQ composite index is observed to occur on average once a year, or once every 250 trading days. Incremental change theory would therefore suggest that two successive days of such drops would only occur once every 250 x 250 trading days, or roughly once in 250 years. In fact, two consecutive days of 5% drops have already happened three times on the NASDAQ, and this is an index which has only been in existence since February 1971. The reason for the discrepancy is that the mathematics that works well for the small changes that occur on 249 days out of 250 do not apply when there is an exceptional change. The critical element is that the forces that cause the index to fall by 5% in a single day invalidate the assumptions that underpin the mathematics of incremental change.

Messes, problems and puzzles

Despite the preceding example from the NASDAQ index and many others like it, people with disruptive problems still follow statisticians like sheep even though the models that they use are based on very many small changes, not on infrequent, large changes. By adopting this approach people are, unwittingly, trying to solve the insoluble. The academic Russell Ackoff gave a succinct explanation of what is going on here by dividing issues into *messes*, *problems* and *puzzles*, which are respective equivalents of the terms *uncertainty*, *risk*, and *certainty* used in this book:

- A *mess* is a complex issue which is not well formulated or defined.

- A *problem* is a well formulated/defined issue, but with no single solution.

- A *puzzle* is a well defined problem with a specific solution which can be worked out.

This classification can be illustrated with the following examples:

For people in a *mess* it is very hard to even know the true nature of the problems faced. Most very large issues in the world start out as messes. A good example of a mess is the national transport policy. What part will be state owned? What will the role be of the private sector and how will the necessary capital be raised? What are the needs of the wide variety of stakeholders from travellers, to shareholders, through to special interest and lobbying groups?

The next level in the hierarchy is a *problem*, where the issue does have a defined structure or form and as a result there are a number of potential solutions, but not one clear-cut way to solve it. Problems have a number of defined variables and it is possible to know something of how they interact and shape things. A good example of a problem is weather forecasting, investment portfolio allocation, or predicting who will win the next election.

The final level is a *puzzle*, which is a well defined issue with a solid structure around it and a specific solution that can be derived. There are a myriad of these and they are encountered and solved on a day-to-day basis. A typical example is working out the cheapest way to travel from London to Newcastle for there are easily available facts about fares and times so that a best answer can be calculated.

Inappropriate in the extreme

Michael Pidd is careful to caution against the use of inappropriate theory: "One of the greatest mistakes that can be made when dealing with a mess is to carve off part of the mess, treat it as a problem and then solve it as a puzzle – ignoring its links with other aspects of the mess." Unfortunately the human desire for a definite answer to difficult issues can provide a strong motivation to rush for the puzzle-solving route and many situations are made far worse by ignoring Pidd's observation that it is mistaken to believe that big problems can be solved by slicing them up into manageable pieces. This may be correct on occasions, but there is the inherent danger of misunderstanding the issue at hand and consequently applying the wrong tools to tackle it.

Much experience in life is built up from a very large number of trivial and humdrum events, and it is a human tendency to base expectations on those events and to ignore, or at least downplay, any extreme events of which there is no direct experience. People assume that extreme events only happen to others. This reflects the very personal way that people view the world, so that for example many members of the armed services have a strong belief they themselves will not be killed in action and if this were not so, presumably few of them would risk fighting.

Turning to the natural world, human attitudes to risk are similarly skewed. Mount Vesuvius is set in extremely beautiful countryside. As a result it has attracted some two million people to live in the immediate vicinity and hundreds of thousands of tourists visit the remains of Pompeii and Herculaneum every year. Of course Vesuvius is also an active volcano capable of inflicting immense damage, but people say "Oh, that is ancient history, it will not happen to me." They are wrong. Vesuvius has erupted several times since its most famous explosion in 79AD, most recently in 1944. When it next switches from incremental to disruptive behaviour, as it will surely do at some point, then everything will be different, and the experiences and collective memory of the previous 50 years will be irrelevant. Once again human judgement will cluster around the short-term comfort of predictable incremental change and relative stability and will erase the past disruptive (and literally explosive) changes that will occur to people who choose to live on the edge of a volcano!

Black swans

Nassim Nicholas Taleb, a writer and academic, has recently drawn attention to improbable events that result from disruptive changes, pointing out that they are both unpredictable and carry massive impact. He believes that they "underlie almost everything about our world" and has dubbed such events *black swans*. This neatly encapsulates the idea of something that, while unlikely, is not impossible. His black swan metaphor has three principal characteristics: these events are unpredictable; they carry a massive impact; and, after the fact, we concoct an explanation for them. Such black swans can be good or bad; the creation of Google was one, but so were the terrorist attacks on the World Trade Center in 2001. Clearly a black swan is a special type of event and no amount of studying the more numerous white swans can enable its behaviour to be predicted.

However, it is important here not to throw out the legitimately incremental baby with the bath water. As the label implies, incremental change happens all the time and in the financial world, for example, related analytical tools such as Value at Risk, option pricers and actuarial tables are valuable. This means that Taleb overstates his case when he says that "much business forecasting is useless", although his principle comes closer to the truth as the timescale increases. For the longer term it is sensible to replace the statistical extrapolations with more flexible statements of intent.

It is important to note that incremental change can exert a greater influence on our lives than disruptive change, although such a conclusion depends on the time span chosen. As David J. Aldous of the Statistics Department at the University of California says:

> A building might be damaged in a few seconds by an earthquake, in a few minutes by a fire, in a few hours by a flood, or in a few decades by termites. The first three are visually dramatic and may affect a large and unpredictable

number of buildings at once; but not so the fourth... the first three appear in the news as natural disasters, but the fourth doesn't. But none of this is relevant to the quantitative impact of such events, which is an empirical matter (termites win). Similarly [the] number of deaths in different wars is [down to black swans]; childhood deaths from poor sanitation and consequent disease is [not]. Guess which caused more deaths worldwide in the twentieth century. That's an empirical matter (poor sanitation wins).

Creative destruction

Disruptive change may only be part of the story and it forces itself to the front of our memories because of its impact and vividness, but it is important nonetheless and is the driving force behind much of our progress. Joseph Schumpeter, an Austrian economist, in his 1942 book *Capitalism, Socialism and Democracy*, described the process where "the opening up of new markets, foreign or domestic, and the organisational development... illustrate the same process of industrial mutation, that incessantly revolutionises the economic structure from within, incessantly destroying the old one, incessantly creating a new one."

In other words, business is a regular stream of disruptive failures followed by rebuilding. He called this process *creative destruction* and believed it to be the essential heart of capitalism, where its economies are punctuated by intermittent disruptions rather than being characterised by steady improvement. This punctuated equilibrium is paralleled by what happens in nature according to the evolutionary biology theory of Eldredge and Gould. They contend that the gradual change commonly attributed to Charles Darwin is not seen in the fossil record. Rather they believe that species which propagate through sexual reproduction generally change little, apart from sporadic rapid changes which are caused by rare localised events. On this basis the progress of capitalism, and indeed much of human progress, mimics that of natural evolution.

An example from the world of big business – the story of Digital Equipment Corp (DEC) – offers interesting insights into the disruptive process at work in commerce.

Disruptions marked the start and end of DEC

Engineer Ken Olsen started DEC in 1958 after observing that students in an MIT laboratory preferred using a simple interacting computer rather than the more powerful batch alternative that was normal in educational establishments at the time. Initially Olsen developed computers with this group as his target market and this enabled his company to establish a niche that was not serviced by the existing computer companies. It quickly set the company on a trajectory towards great success, which it enjoyed for a time, but which also contained the seeds of its eventual failure.

From the early beginnings to satisfy the computer needs of lab technicians, Olsen built a company that could attack the mainframe companies on their own turf and become, in 1986, the second largest computer company in the world. Then things started to go awry. Until it moved into the general market, DEC could offer its technically-oriented market bigger and better versions of what had gone before, but now they found that the general market wanted the technically unsophisticated but ubiquitous IBM personal computer. DEC was not equipped to move in that direction and after Olsen had declared in 1977 that "there is no reason for any individual to have a computer in his home", they were slow to even try.

It was too late when DEC started work on its response to IBM, based upon their own RISC (Reduced Instruction Set Computer) design, and their corporate culture was not suited to the task. Eventually a single project was assembled from previously competing factions, but the design was not finalised until 1988 and cancelled soon afterwards. The head of that project, Dave Cutler, left DEC in 1988 and joined Microsoft to lead development on Windows NT. Ken Olsen stepped down in 1992 and his successor was given five years to dismantle the company, a task which was completed in 1998, when what then remained of the firm was purchased by Compaq.

What had gone wrong after such an innovative and groundbreaking beginning?

The life of DEC illustrates not one, but two, Schumpeter cycles. In the mid-1980s, clustered mini-computers of DEC destroyed mainframe computers and then they were destroyed in turn in the mid-1990s by personal computers. In each case newcomers destroyed the apparently secure incumbents.

Harvard business professor, Clayton Christensen, in his 1997 book *The Innovator's Dilemma*, extended Schumpeter's concept to describe the pattern in the emergence of disruptive technologies that he called *disruptive innovation*. Disruptive innovation relates to a process by which a product or service takes root initially in simple applications at the bottom of a market (in DEC's case laboratory computers) and then moves up market (in DEC's case to corporate business processing), eventually displacing established competitors, such as IBM and Univac. DEC's problem was that in the second cycle, it was the victim not the winner. This time the simple applications were on the IBM PC and that solution moved up market when they could be linked together within local area networks. At this point they could successfully challenge DEC's super-minis.

When a large company such as DEC looks at new developments, it typically asks for opinions from its existing customer base. They generally want more of the same but faster and cheaper. They never suggest disruptive innovation, because they are users and cannot envisage what major changes are technically possible. The company keeps on investing in the traditional technology, the resulting performance improvement of the traditional technology is highly appreciated by existing customers and a lot of money is made. Meanwhile, a disgruntled employee such as Dave Cutler leaves for an employer with a new vision, in his case Microsoft, taking his skill and experience with him.

Alternatively, employees might leave as a group to start new companies, which also happened with DEC. The new companies implement their ideas that their previous employer had unconsciously stifled and new markets emerge by trial and error. The successful new players move up in the market, the performance of the new technologies improves, enabling them to compete with ever increasing success against the traditional company and its product. The incumbent employs old technology to try to compete with the completely different concepts employed by the new competitors, which is the corporate equivalent of fighting the last war.

Failure Is Likely

Disruptive change has always been a force which has moved civilisation forward, but prior to the twentieth century its effects were spasmodic and progress was slow. One of the main reasons was because very few people could spare the time to just sit and think up new ways of doing things and even fewer could afford to test their ideas. Disruptive change is unpredictable and so success can never be guaranteed, meaning that the risk taker always needs a safety net.

Amazon's founder Jeff Bezos put it rather nicely at the Wired 'Disruptive by Design' Conference in June 2009:

> There are a few prerequisites to inventing... You have to be willing to fail. You have to be willing to think long term. You have to be willing to be misunderstood for long periods of time. If you can't do those three things, you need to limit yourself to sustaining innovation.

A long flight path

In early nineteenth century Britain, wealthy landowners were the main class with the time and resources to take such risks and Sir George Cayley, a Yorkshire MP and local squire, was just such an archetypal inventor. In a lifetime of tinkering and innovation, Cayley investigated self-righting lifeboats, tension-spoke wheels, track-laying vehicles, seat belts, automatic signals for railway crossings and even small-scale helicopters. However, more importantly, he has a very strong claim to be the father of aviation, some 50 years before the Wright brothers had their spectacular success at Kitty Hawk in North Carolina in 1903. Cayley first set down the principles of flight in a treatise entitled 'On Aerial Navigation' and in 1853, to demonstrate the principles, he built a glider which flew for 300 yards across Brompton Dale. Perhaps he was not completely sure of the success of the venture, because rather than risking making the flight himself, his coachman was selected as the pilot.

Cayley recognised that to complete his flying machine he needed a power source, but having dismissed the only viable candidate of the time – the steam engine – as "too weighty and cumbrous", he experimented with an internal gradual combustion engine and an explosive engine powered by gunpowder. Neither reached the stage where they could power an aeroplane and so he abandoned the project. So whilst he had laid the groundwork for an enormous disruptive change, he didn't actually create the all-important breakthrough. That had to wait for other experimenters to develop the internal combustion engine, allowing the Wright brothers to marry the discoveries together 50 years later when they inaugurated powered flight at Kitty Hawk. Cayley's experience demonstrates a recurring theme – that individuals or organisations with spare time and money are those best placed to experiment with disruptive technologies and change, but often the change takes more than one step to realise.

Whilst the lone maverick inventor working in the garage on a spectacular breakthrough is the common cliché, the reality is that today most disruptive breakthroughs come about within organisations or companies. They alone can supply the resources, usually both time and money, and often access to specialists that are outside the scope of a lone individual. So nowadays it tends to be a company with deep pockets that provides the safety net that was previously the preserve of the rich amateur or enthusiast.

Corporate disruption

To develop the right conditions for success, paradoxically any company embarking on developing new ideas must acknowledge the uncertainty of disruptive innovation and recognise that there could be failure and a financial loss. It is also important that the company should protect its staff from the resulting upheaval. The person who is asked to manage a disruptive innovation on the company's behalf, should do so on the understanding that failure is likely and in which case no blame is attached and it is not reason to criticise, demote or otherwise punish the person.

As we have seen, DEC's growth in the mid-1980s severely damaged the computer mainframe market and gave IBM what the company itself referred to as a "near death experience" in the early 1990s. IBM recognised that despite its huge size it had to be nimbler and able to react to Schumpeter events. So in 2000 it established what it calls EBOs (Emerging-Business Opportunities) under Bruce Harreld, then Senior VP for Strategy. The mission was to find new business opportunities that went beyond product upgrades and straightforward technical advances. So far the programme has been an extraordinary success, creating multi-billion-dollar businesses in Life Sciences, Linux, Pervasive Computing and Digital Media. Of course not every one of the EBO initiatives has been a success – a couple of projects for example were hit by the bursting of the dotcom bubble in 2001.

Critically, when a pilot project doesn't work, the EBO is quickly killed and the person who took the risk is found another important post within IBM: "You want to celebrate failure because you learn something. It's harder to do that early in your career. You need some level of security to say, 'I screwed it up,' and be comfortable that you're not going to get fired," says Harreld. This is an important lesson, because no one will take any form of risk if the prevailing atmosphere is to shoot the messenger.

All of the outcomes must be examined when assessing a programme of innovation or new thinking – not just the successes – and it must be acknowledged that component failure is an inevitable part of overall programme success.

Governmental disruption

Of course the government is an institution that can afford to fail, because through the taxation system it has access to everyone's pockets, both deep and shallow. Over the years governments around the globe have run innovative projects, often ones which the private sector would not or could not take up. Because access to the taxation base offers such a comprehensive safety net, it adds a whole new set of dangers that are unique to projects undertaken by government. Typical problems include late delivery, often at a very high cost and well beyond initial estimates and budgets, or quite often the project fails completely. Professor D. R. Myddelton of the Institute of Economic Affairs has analysed a number of such UK projects in 'They Meant Well: Government Project Disasters'. In this article he examined a number of governmental projects that over a long period of time, for a number of different reasons, failed to fulfil their objectives, or overran budget, or timescale, or all three.

Cautionary tales of governmental failures

The roll call of UK government failures is chastening (or it should be!) and somewhat depressing for the taxpayer. Myddelton found that the Groundnut Scheme, set up in 1946 in what is now Tanzania, failed completely after it was undertaken with no pilot feasibility study and was controlled remotely from London. In 1958 the government embarked on a Nuclear Power Generation scheme which was set up on a cost plus basis, charging for the electricity generated, thus removing from the project any economic controls. Needless to say the financial effects were very painful. Although widely admired, the Concorde aircraft (for which development began in 1958) suffered from the dangerous flaw of being a national prestige project with a "reckless failure to even care whether or not there was a market".

The more recent problems when digging the Channel Tunnel in 1985 are described in detail in Chapter 6, but in summary there was no high speed rail link when it opened, the costs were twice the original budget, while demand was only half of what was expected. And of course no list is complete without the Millennium Dome, which had a very shaky launch, upsetting journalists on the opening night and receiving poor press thereafter. All of which led to costs overrunning by nearly tenfold and the project becoming a byword for failed projects. The Dome has subsequently been revived in commercial hands, though only after a billion pounds of UK taxpayer's money had been blown!

It is good to remember that such failings are not the exclusive preserve of government, for similar failures can plague any large organisation or company, in particular ones with a monopoly or near monopoly position. Governments have more than their fair share of failures because politicians are attracted to grandiose schemes that through their very size cause trouble and because such large schemes are often outside the scope of the private sector. All large-scale ventures are prone to some general problems as they are usually dependent on new, untried technology, which makes costs and timescales extremely uncertain. In such an environment there are unavoidable changes in specifications, which add further costs and delays.

The additional dangers that are particularly associated with government are pretty easy to spot. As with the Concorde aircraft, government often feels it necessary to boost national prestige, a concept which never adds much to the coffers but is very costly. Initial financial estimates may be purposely set low for political reasons, which the government is able to do because, in the absence of market pressures, there are no accounting checks and balances.

Inevitably state projects are subject to short-term political interference and changes halfway through a project can add a massive increase in costs. To complicate matters further, a government's accounting practices often disguise the true level of state spending on large projects. There is no need for governments to understand markets and all too often there is little effort to research likely customer demand. Furthermore, governments often choose to continue projects even after it has become clear they are not commercially viable. Politicians as a breed seem particularly ill-suited to overseeing large complex projects – they tend to either install inadequate or over-complex organisations, appoint incompetent managers, and frequently are guilty of insisting on excessive secrecy.

* * *

To recap, failure is an inevitable danger when new things are tried and so a flexible and agile mindset is needed. Many big organisations, particularly governments, find such an attitude to be unnatural, since all of their efficiencies of scale are linked to the inflexible routines which enable the top people to enforce a corporate way of working. There can clearly be

" Failure is an inevitable danger when new things are tried and so a flexible and agile mindset is needed. "

no routine for something that has never been done before. Similarly, people who work for large organisations by choice enjoy the stability that routine brings and would feel uncomfortable if their objectives were forever being changed. So not only does the development of something new require a specific management style, but additionally all those who work in such an environment must be comfortable in the face of uncertainty. Such people share a number of other traits that together define creative types.

Creative Types

Creative people pull in a different direction to the rest of the world – they are not part of steady incremental development – and so they are often seen as difficult and impossible to manage. In the area of popular music there are regular stories in the media of arguments and fights between band members over the inevitable musical differences. In business it's no different, but here the battles are usually over patents and technical principles.

War of the Currents

One vignette that shows how such disputes can dominate the business of invention is the War of the Currents between Thomas Edison and his erstwhile assistant Nikola Tesla. Edison has a huge list of achievements to his name, registering more than a thousand patents, and he spent a lifetime developing these ideas. Out of this huge activity one of his most successful businesses was electricity generation and its sale to customers to power Edison lightbulbs in houses, factories, etc. To develop this business he employed Tesla, who hailed from Serbia and was himself a technical genius, but Edison cheated him. After frequent disputes, Tesla left Edison's employment and joined the rival firm of George Westinghouse, taking with him patents for the AC (alternating current) distribution system. Edison had developed and used DC (direct current) distribution for which he had registered patents to protect his business interests, and was determined see off Westinghouse and Tesla.

AC is today the universal choice for power distribution, being technically superior, because it is simple to transform from the high voltage needed for efficient transmission over long distances to the low voltage required for safe domestic use. At the time though, Edison was not going to give up DC without a fight. The ensuing battle became notorious for the disinformation spread by Edison concerning the perceived dangers of AC electricity.

Aggressively promoting his own DC system and attempting to sow the idea that AC was dangerous, Edison used AC electricity to kill animals, and even went as far as secretly to pay the inventor of the AC powered electric chair.

The Westinghouse Electric and Manufacturing Company got into financial difficulties as a result of defending itself in these wars, with the result that Edison triumphed and Tesla died a pauper. However, Edison's victory was short-lived, as in time the manifest advantages of the AC system overtook his much-promoted DC system. As a final irony one of the relatively few honours that Tesla received in his lifetime was the Edison Medal, awarded to him by the Institute of Electrical and Electronics Engineers in 1916.

Inventors are different

As we discussed earlier, general schooling, which is geared for the majority, frequently seems not to suit inventors. In Thomas Edison's case his teacher dismissed him as addle brained and he left formal education after just three months. However, since disruptive change is regarded as such an important engine of progress, these days industry is keen to find these rare and valuable creative and inventive types. In the metaphor introduced earlier, they are looking for right-brain people. But how to do so?

The first who applied scientific methods to the problem was the Victorian polymath Sir Francis Galton (1822-1911). He devised various measures of intellectual functioning using statistical methods, making him an originator of psychometric approaches in creativity research. Moving up to date, it is estimated that today some 80% of *Fortune 500* companies and 75% of *Times 100* companies use psychometric tests to assist them in their search for staff. These tests split into two forms; one type consists of aptitude and ability tests that measure left-brain skills, whilst the second type are personality and interest tests that measure the right-brain characteristics. Creativity is not correlated with the speed of solving verbal and/or mathematical multiple-choice problems and so aptitude and ability tests are not appropriate. Rather personality tests must be used to find people with the capacity for the novel and appropriate problem-solving skills that creativity requires.

Adaptors, innovators and the big five factors

Michael Kirton, a British psychologist, tackles the problem of how to find these people by providing an instrument which measures a person's preferred style of defining and solving problems, without measuring their aptitude for such tasks. At one extreme are the *adaptors*, who are people who like to do things better and at the other end are the *innovators*, who are people who like to do things differently. An adaptor is efficient, thorough, adaptable, methodical, organised, precise, reliable, dependable, and is respectful of rules and structure. An innovator is ingenious, original, independent, unconventional, is less tolerant of structure (guidelines, rules) and less respectful of consensus. Thus adaptors and innovators reflect the left-brain right-brain metaphor. In practice, everyone falls somewhere within the two extremes and their position indicates no more than their *preferred* mode of working, not an outright declaration of what they can or cannot do. We will come to look at Kirton's work again in Chapter 6, when we consider how a team charged with innovation should be put together.

Popular alternatives to Kirton's methods of attempting to identify creative people early are the personality tests based on what psychometricians call the *big five* factors, namely: extraversion (how energetic one is); agreeableness (one's level of orientation towards other people); conscientiousness (how structured one is); neuroticism (tendency to worry); and openness to experience (tendency to be speculative and imaginative). A number of studies have been made to compare the two approaches. For example, a total of 206 polytechnic students from Singapore completed self-report questionnaires for both Kirton and big five tests. It was found that adaptors were significantly more conscientious, whilst innovators were significantly more extraverted and open to experience. This and other experiments have found further correlations, but they are less clear-cut.

If psychometric tests can help to spot individual creative people, it is natural to wonder if it can provide guidance to find whole groups who might tend towards creativity. The most obvious grouping is by gender and to examine whether females are naturally more creative than males. One simple measurement of this is to look at patent filings, but this unfortunately does not give a definitive answer.

Gender bias?

In America, the first female to file a patent was Mary Keis in 1809, for "straw weaving with silk and thread". The records show that between 1790 and 1895 only one patent in a hundred included a female patentee; from 1905 to 1921 the percentage rose to 1.4%, by 1977 the figure had risen to 2.6% and in 1996 to 9.2%. The fact that between 1790 and 1984 only 1.5% of US patents included a female would suggest that females are inherently not inventive. On the other hand, the percentage rose from 1% to 9.2% over a period which saw women playing an increasing part in public life, suggesting that the difference between the sexes has more to do with social roles than fundamental creative traits. So until men and women have enjoyed parity of opportunity over a long period, it will not be possible to conclude from patent records that one sex or the other has the edge. One indication that there is a gender bias that could be related to creativity comes from Kirton's instrument, where men obtain a higher score than women, indicating that men are more innovative and risk taking, while women are more adaptive and risk averse.

What is clear is that demands for creativity are ever expanding, but that only a few are blessed with the right combination of characteristics to be creative. Whilst there are no formal statistics giving the exact split between those with the required traits to be an inventor and everyone else, those with the right characteristics are almost certainly in the minority.

Accumulate To Speculate

Stockbrokers and turf accountants exhort their customers to speculate in order to accumulate, but in fact it is only those that have already accumulated that can afford to speculate. Why so?

As noted earlier, it is not enough to have a creative mind. One also needs resources, usually time and money, to provide the right environment to convert bright ideas into actual new products and services. It is also important to be in the right place at the right time, for the most productive individuals and groups are in communities where the maximum number of people have the resources and the legal backup to protect their ideas.

Sir James Dyson, whose vacuum cleaners now dominate the UK and US markets, is a rare British technology entrepreneur who is recognisable to

> **The most productive individuals and groups are in communities where the maximum number of people have the resources and the legal backup to protect their ideas.**

the general public. He believes that disdain for technologists is a fatal flaw in the British character and this is reflected in low levels of patent registrations and weaker economic performance. This may be true today, but from the time of the Agricultural Revolution and the building of its empire through to the Industrial Revolution, Britain was a hotbed of invention.

Three centuries of invention in Britain

The importance of surplus resources is illustrated through the experience of Britain from around the early 1700s onwards. First came the Agricultural Revolution, the benefits of which can be gauged from wheat yields, which grew by almost 60% from 1720 to the 1840s. The improved farming methods, coupled with the benefits derived from sugar imports and the absence of outside disruption, supported an ever growing population. At the same time the Enclosures Acts created a new class of landless labourers who needed to earn a living. Some worked in their own cottages, which was a major step towards the Industrial Revolution, while others went to the colonies where they performed similar agricultural wonders.

The Agricultural Revolution provided both a carrot and a stick for the Industrial Revolution. A smaller number of farm workers could produce enough to feed the increased population and at the same time there were a large number of displaced farm workers with nothing to do. It represented an ideal time for wealthy people to diversify into commercial ventures and they felt confident to do so because they were in a political environment that had been stable since the Glorious Revolution of 1688. The ventures enjoyed the benefit of a large, increasingly prosperous domestic market that could be easily reached within the small, densely-populated island. Also to Britain's benefit was that other countries were at a relative disadvantage, since there the population was more thinly spread and often, for example in France, they were split up into regions, which imposed internal tolls and tariffs on goods traded between each other.

The seventeenth century onwards was also a time of great colonial expansion for Britain. This encouraged the development of international trade, the creation of financial markets and so the accumulation of further capital. As the British merchant class became stronger, trade was liberalised and was at an advantage relative to countries where trade and other innovations were stifled by totalitarian governments, such as the absolute monarchies of China and Russia. Britain's advantages over India in this period illustrate the point.

When Britain arrived in India, it found a country split up into many competing fiefdoms under absolute monarchs, each of whom possessed immense personal wealth. The local economies were highly dependent on two sectors – subsistence agriculture and cotton – and there was little or no technical innovation. When Britain ruled India there were ample opportunities to modernise the sub-continent and ensure that a steady flow of wealth went back to the home country. The Marxist historian Rajani Palme Dutt said: "The capital to finance the Industrial Revolution in India instead went into financing the Industrial Revolution in England."

Britain enjoyed one final piece of good fortune. The coal and iron that industry needed were to hand. As the Industrial Revolution developed, British manufactured output surged ahead of other economies and the advantage lasted for as long as Britain accumulated surplus capital. The purple period came to an end in the twentieth century after the draining effects of two world wars.

Once it had started, the Industrial Revolution was self sustaining as the profits generated provided yet more capital to finance further inventions and other disruptive changes, but something more was needed to ensure that the progress was safeguarded. For any inventive culture to prosper there needs to be a strong legal framework, for without intellectual property law there is no incentive to invent, and certainly not to publicise any invention.

The ownership of ideas

In 1623, England made the first tentative steps towards an intellectual property law, when the government enacted the Statute of Monopolies, which granted limited monopolies to inventors and is seen as the origin of patent law. While generally condemning unfettered monopolies, it provided the true and first inventor of a given item up to 14 years of exclusive rights to their invention, provided that "they be not contrary to the law nor mischievous to the state by raising prices of commodities at home, or hurt of trade, or generally inconvenient".

Recognising that a person could own an idea was a vital step to promote technological progress, for patents encourage the inventor, but nevertheless even their limited nature can still delay progress. In return for publicly revealing the workings of the steam engine, James Watt was awarded a patent. This allowed him to monopolise the production of the first steam engines and benefit greatly from his invention. However, his monopoly prevented other inventors, such as Richard Trevithick, from introducing improved steam engines, thereby delaying key enabling technology and slowing the arrival of more efficient steam power by up to 20 years.

Patents and medicine

A more modern illustration of the positive and the negative value of the patent is provided by the fight against AIDS. In 1996, an effective patented therapy that delays the onset of AIDS became available. Within four years, death rates for people with HIV/AIDS in developed countries had dropped by 84%, but at a cost of US$10,000-15,000 per person per year, these drugs were far too expensive for the majority of HIV infected people in poor countries.

An Indian pharmaceutical company, ignoring the patent, started to provide an equivalent therapy with generic versions of the drugs. These drugs are exactly the same as those made by large pharmaceutical companies, but significantly cheaper. By 2001 the cost dropped to US$295 per person per year and most recently to US$88 per person per year. As a consequence, four million people in poorer countries are currently receiving drugs to treat HIV/AIDS that would previously not have been possible. On the other hand, the pharmaceutical companies argue that they need patent protection and that generic copying decreases the amount of money they can spend on researching and developing new drugs.

This is particularly significant with HIV treatment programmes as 10-15% of people taking the current drugs will develop resistance to them within four to five years and the pharmaceutical companies are in an expensive ongoing battle to develop new drugs in order to stay ahead of the disease. The next generation solution has already been developed but the annual cost is thousands of dollars per person, once again putting it out of the reach of poorer nations.

The dilemma posed by patents is particularly acute with medical cures since many people's lives are at stake. Without patents people have no incentive to make new discoveries, but with them some people are excluded from the inventions of others. Thomas Jefferson believed that the disadvantages of patents outweighed their advantages. He said:

> He who receives an idea from me, receives instruction himself without lessening mine; as he who lights his taper at mine, receives light without darkening me. That ideas should freely spread from one to another over the globe, for the moral and mutual instruction of man, and improvement of his condition, seems to have been peculiarly and benevolently designed by nature.

Cayley, the father of aeronautics, shared the same opinion saying that "freedom is the essence of improvement in science", but then as a gentleman of independent means he could afford to take that position.

Intellectual property in the developing world

The World Trade Organisation sides with the British view and supports temporary state-enforced monopolies, but it is not the case universally. In sub-Saharan Africa today there is not even *physical* property law. Seventy per cent of the urban population has no legal right to the land they occupy and this land generally lacks basic services such as water supply and sanitation. The squatters have no incentive to rectify this shortcoming, since they could lose their property overnight. Meanwhile public and private providers do not feel obliged to step in on behalf of illegal occupants. Without the security of ownership, progress stalls and inventiveness disappears.

Robert Fisk of the *Independent* newspaper puzzled over the lack of growth in the Arab world, which with oil revenues is certainly not short of capital. He pointed out that between 1980 and 2004 their average annual real GDP per capita only grew by 0.5%, a figure which was bettered in 2008 by almost all non-Arab countries. His assessment was that "a real problem exists in the mind of Arabs; they do not feel that they own their countries. Unable, for the most part, to elect real representatives – even in Lebanon, outside the tribal or sectarian context – they feel ruled over". He concludes: "At Cairo University far too many wanted to move to the West. The Koran may be an invaluable document – but so is a Green Card." In these days of high mobility, if a country does not provide a satisfactory environment, then ambitious people will move out – what is termed *brain drain* – and apply their ingenuity to the benefit of their new hosts.

It is the environment rather than innate ability of the population that matters, despite the opinion of Bertrand Russell that the Mohammedans and the Byzantines were "lacking the intellectual energy required for innovation". During what the Western world called the Dark Ages (400 to 1000AD) a prosperous empire developed in the Middle East and this provided the

> **" The threat of war and the need to defend against aggressors always provides an incentive, together with the necessary funds, to foster new ideas. "**

financial funding, if not the intellectual property protection, to enable it to bridge the gap between the Greek civilisation and the Renaissance. Amongst the many inventions from that region, in that period, are the flying machine, pointed arch, herbal medicine, crystal glass, optics, the pinhole camera and the application of experimental techniques in science.

These last three developments came from a single man, Ibn al-Haythan (965-1041), who has been called the first true scientist. He born in Basra and from there he proposed a solution to the regular flooding caused by the Nile to the sixth ruler of the Fatimid caliphate Al-Hakim bi-Amr Allah in Cairo. His solution was to construct water defences very close to the site of the present Aswan Dam, but when he saw the situation on the ground he realised that it was quite impractical with the resources that the caliph had offered. This posed a problem since the violent caliph was not a man to let down. Haythan's solution was to feign madness. For that, he was placed under house arrest, which enabled him to retire from engineering and devote himself to science. In the following ten years of peace and quiet he wrote his best known work, *Book of Optics*, confirming the importance of environment to the inventive mind.

In countries with sufficient capital reserves and an adequate legal system, existing organisations adapt, or new ones spring up, to provide environments that are suitable for inventors. Large technical universities provide office space, handle patent applications and manage company spin-offs. Boutique pharmaceutical companies conduct research, invent drugs, test them, get them approved and then sell the rights on to the major companies which possess the necessary manufacturing premises, and worldwide marketing and distribution facilities.

Some companies set up purpose-built industrial research laboratories, the first of which was established in 1876 in Menlo Park, New Jersey, and was the base from which Edison waged the War of the Currents. Governments and international organisations set up research laboratories to encourage development that they consider important, but which private enterprise is ignoring. British scientist Sir Tim Berners-Lee was working at CERN (European Organisation for Nuclear Research) when he created the World Wide Web.

The threat of war

The threat of war and the need to defend against aggressors always provides an incentive, together with the necessary funds, to foster new ideas. The results of such ventures remain hidden from general view for a long time but eventually emerge. Nikola Tesla, the father of AC electricity, had ideas for a Death Ray machine which in 1934 were published in a New York newspaper. The Air Ministry in Britain wondered whether such a device could be used against aircraft. The technical experts replied that such a device would be impractical but that "although it was impossible to destroy aircraft by means of radio waves, it should be possible to detect them by radio energy bouncing back from the aircraft's body." This idea was quickly pursued and the first practical radar for the detection of aircraft was demonstrated by Sir Robert Watson-Watt of the National Physical Laboratory in 1935. In the Second World War the invention provided the science behind a ring of detection stations called the Chain Home on the east and south coast of the UK.

The British scientists Henry Boot and John T. Randall working at Birmingham University discovered a major improvement to radar, and they forwarded this knowledge to the United States as part of the Tizard Mission in 1940. There the Radiation Laboratory at MIT was set up to manufacture the improved devices and from those beginnings, radar became widely used in air and sea transport and other applications. One amusing story regards the police force's use of radar to detect speeding cars. One victim of this was none other than Watson-Watt, who said to the policemen when he was stopped, "Had I known what you were going to do with it I would never have invented it!"

* * *

Edison believed that invention was 1% invention and 99% perspiration. This section shows that the breakdown is more like 1% invention, 33% perspiration, 33% money and 33% rule of law.

Upstarts Rock The Boat

In *The Prince* in 1513 Niccolo Machiavelli's advice on statecraft was that changes are generally unpopular. He wrote:

> The innovator makes enemies of all those who prospered under the old order, and only lukewarm support is forthcoming from those who would prosper under the new.

The picture in business nearly 500 years later is no different. In particular, established manufacturers who prosper under the old order have no reason to risk change. Without any external pressure, their preferred route is to proceed slowly while making gradual changes, such as adding new sales regions, making minor enhancements to the product, or improving manufacturing techniques. An example of this mindset was the UK system of Resale Price Maintenance (RPM), which was in place until the mid-1960s. This allowed manufacturers to control tightly the prices their goods were sold for through distributors and was popular with existing businesses because it kept out newcomers.

The justification claimed for the system was that without RPM, some customers would go to a full service supplier to learn about a product's special features and then buy the item from a discount retailer. This would lead firstly to failure of the full service suppliers and then to the failure of the discount retailers because no potential customers would understand the products. To independent observers this can be seen as a flimsy argument in order to maintain a cosy deal between the manufacturer and retailer that eliminates price competition and discourages innovations which make products cheaper to produce. Like any convenient barrier to entry, the removal of RPM was never going to be sponsored by the established players.

A new spin on consumer products

John Bloom was certainly not an established player when he set out to transform the UK washing machine market. Initially he worked as a salesman for a company selling Dutch-made washing machines door-to-door at half the high street retailer prices and within a short time period he had taken 10% of the market from the established manufacturers. Encouraged by this success, Bloom did a deal with the failing Rolls Razor Company to make twin-tub washing machines. By 1963 the company was selling over 200,000 machines a year and listed on the London Stock Exchange. But the retailers and the manufacturers fought back in what became known as the *washing machine war*, eventually forcing Bloom's company into voluntary liquidation in July 1964. In the short term the established players had won, but the analysts were less happy. *The Economist* commented at the time:

> Before his [John Bloom's] arrival manufacturers tried to sell at the highest possible prices the appliances they found it most convenient to make, competing mainly on advertising claims of better performance and new technical tricks. Over a time the consumer gets more performance for his money, at each conventional price level, but what he did not get was a chance to buy a given grade of machine cheaper.

Harold Wincott of the *Financial Times* wrote, "if established industry is too solidly wedded to price maintenance, we need more John Blooms not fewer of them" and in a letter to *The Times*, Ralph Harris, Director of the Institute of Economic Affairs wrote "Mr. Bloom has already done more for economic growth in Britain than many of its verbal champions in NEDC (National Economic Development Council) and elsewhere". John Bloom's battle was lost, but the consumers' war was won when RPM was abandoned in May 1964.

Mortgage innovation ends on the rocks

In Chapter 2 we described how well intentioned, but misguided, US politicians distorted their housing market, resulting in financial chaos that spread across the whole world. In the UK, changes to the law caused a similar upheaval as the transformed building society sector played the upstarts in the banking world. Until the mid-1980s building societies were mutual organisations entirely owned by their members and they dominated mortgage lending, which was a steady, unexciting business. Disruption came to this rather dull part of the financial markets with the 1986 Building Societies Act, which opened the way for demutualisation and gave the societies the opportunity to become banks.

Under the old rules the building societies were restricted by law as to how much they could borrow on the money market. They were capped at 50% of total borrowings with the rest having to come from their savers, and in the rather sleepy environment before the legislative change the societies often only borrowed around 30% from sources other than their deposit base. The new legislation removed this cap, as banks have no percentage limit on how much they borrow from other banks. In the new regime, the newly coined *mortgage banks* could be creative in order to attract business in what had become a highly competitive market.

One such upstart was Northern Rock, which fatally chose to initiate aggressive expansion plans built upon borrowing from the capital markets. In October 2006, it announced its strategic intention to grow assets and profits at 20% per year. It would achieve these ambitious plans by creating an organisation called Granite, based in Guernsey, which would parcel up Northern Rock's mortgages and sell the bundles on to investors. The sales pitch to the investors was that the bundles had lower risk than an individual mortgage, which has been shown already to be a dangerous assumption if the borrowers are not truly independent of each other (as they are not when they are all hit by the same external force).

The practical outcome of this approach was that Northern Rock was getting its funding from the wholesale markets rather than the small savers of yore. However, the wholesale money markets are much more volatile, providing huge amounts when the going is good, indicated by a good credit agency rating, but demanding higher rates and so, practically speaking, withdrawing funds when the going is bad. In the case of Northern Rock, its ambition was rewarded a year later by failure as it became an early casualty of the US mortgage crisis when loans became more expensive, squeezing profit margins at the company. Here the disruption that had started with the new legislation had a long lasting impact for it was some 21 years between the law change and the failure of one of the most aggressive new mortgage banks.

In Summary

Disruptive change is not simply a magnified incremental change and it should not be treated as such. While it is human nature to prefer the routine and ignore inconvenient upsets to the old order, it is dangerous to do so. Black swans may be rare, but they do exist and they should be dealt with as special cases when they arise, for the world of messes, problems and puzzles is not an appropriate place to make simplifications.

> **"** Disruptive change should be treated with respect rather than fear, because it is creative disruption that drives progress. **"**

Disruptive change should be treated with respect rather than fear, because it is creative disruption that drives progress. Remember the story of the DEC, which disrupted the world of the computer mainframe and then was itself destroyed by a further disruption caused by networked personal computers. In the wider scheme of things, although DEC is no more, computing made great strides forward as a result of both events.

Disruptive change brings the likelihood of failure, since no one can be quite sure where the development will lead. Consequently, as we have seen, invention – driving disruptive change – is usually the province of rich individuals, companies with a cash cow, or governments of prosperous countries. A disruptive change brings with it the small chance of bringing great prosperity to its exploiter and it is this carrot which makes the risk of failure worth taking. This chance of prosperity is lost unless there is a stable liberal government with satisfactory intellectual property laws to protect the risk taker from stealers of ideas.

Even in an ideal incubator, disruptions will only be triggered by those rare people with a suitable personality for creativity, who often have some further incentive such as the threat from an enemy during wartime, or the need to break into an established market for the first time. Historical examples of disruptive changes demonstrate their unpredictability and the decades-long chain of consequences that can result. Some examples of this unpredictability and the chains of consequences will be examined in the next chapter.

Cascades
And Consequences

4

It is too early to say.

Chinese Premier Zhou Enlai (1898-1976) commenting on the effects of the French Revolution in 1971

It is clear that no changes, whether disruptive or incremental, act in isolation. The world we live in is comprised of the natural world, manmade things and human institutions; all of which are connected. These three elements and the connections between them are in a constant state of flux. The complexity of these connections and relationships is so great that it is impossible to foresee all of the possible outcomes and so we are constantly being surprised by unexpected chains of consequences. In addition, manmade things that facilitate further connections, like transport and means of communication, act as multipliers and are responsible for some of the longest and most complex chains.

This chapter looks at some of the chains that flow from disruptive change and what lessons they hold for the future. In broad terms there is a pattern to events; a stable period suddenly experiences a form of disruption and then after the initial shock – which need not be negative, but could be positive such as a new invention – there is a series of smaller incremental changes. Such incremental changes may take a very

> **In broad terms there is a pattern to events; a stable period suddenly experiences a form of disruption and then after the initial shock there is a series of smaller incremental changes.**

long time to emerge, producing a long tail of consequences, particularly if the initial disruption was large and game changing. It is important to realise that although individually insignificant, the incremental changes, by their persistent nature, can be responsible for significant change in the long term. To illustrate this ripple effect of change, we look at some disruptive game changers from the past in this chapter. We do this by breaking up some key changes into categories of change with fortuitous consequences and change with negative consequences. We also take a look in detail about two of the most disruptive changes of the last 150 years – the motorcar and the internet.

In the case of all of the disruptive changes we discuss the effects still being felt, which supports the quote from Premier Zhou Enlai given at the start of the chapter – the full meaning and consequence of these disruptive events may not have been fully realised yet.

Echoing Down The Years

A vehicle for change

In 1885 Karl Benz built the first practical petrol driven motorcar and set in train a massive disruptive change that continues to reverberate to this day. Benz's first commercial car went into production in 1888 and he settled back and waited expectantly for orders, but he was surprised to find that they did not arrive. Critically, he had overlooked the promotion needed to launch his new invention, for which there was no existing market. Also, to the general public his car looked too dangerous a contraption. Benz's wife Bertha, who had faith in her husband's creative skills but not his commercial and promotional abilities, took things into her own hands, borrowing the car and driving it with her two teenage sons 60 miles to her mother's house and returning the following day.

Frau Benz, at a stroke, ignited the huge disruptive explosion in personal travel, for she rightly guessed that such a journey would catch the public's imagination and get the fledgling business moving. This it surely did, but whether she realised what she started is unlikely, bearing in mind that her journey was in a three-wheeled converted horse cart, with solid tyres, one gear and steered by tiller. Not quite the practical solution that was to follow after a few years of development.

What is more, the only way to refuel was to go the chemist and buy a cleaning fluid called ligroin (a hydrocarbon petroleum fraction), which was the only available fuel to power the car. The great inventor had chosen three wheels for the vehicle because he had not at that time devised the geometry necessary to steer two front wheels. As a result, the rear wheels could run in the grooves made by horse carts but the front wheel was forced to bump along on the rough ground in the middle. Frau Benz's epic journey in the first ever motorcar must have been a very difficult physical challenge and most uncomfortable to boot, so to honour her memory this historic journey is remembered every two years with a motor rally retracing the route of her first trip.

From this tentative start there was an endless stream of incremental improvements to the engine, gears and suspension, development and distribution of specialist fuels, the expansion of the road networks, and every other element that makes up our motoring experience today. In parallel, the motorcar, van and lorry revolutionised the way everyone lives, enabling people to live further from their place of work, suppliers to deliver goods to distant customers, holidays to be taken at exotic locations and leisure pursuits to be followed far from home. Along the way, road transport severely damaged the economic viability of railways and altered the balance between town and country.

> " It is a striking example of how things can unfold when one man and his wife in Mannheim, Germany, could set in motion a train of events which has affected the lives of everyone in the modern world. "

It is a striking example of how things can unfold when one man and his wife in Mannheim, Germany, could set in motion a train of events which has affected the lives of everyone in the modern world, but it is by no means a unique story.

Connecting the world

Probably one of the greatest disruptive changes in the last 50 years has been the explosion in communication, computing and electronics. Back in the early 1960s computers were very expensive and difficult to use, housed in air-conditioned rooms and operated by specially trained staff. In the very early days, university, government agency and commercial researchers interacted with computers by submitting jobs on paper tape or punched cards. The first great step forward was when the time-sharing computers introduced by DEC (see Chapter 3) enabled the researchers to access a small slice of a large computer through a dumb terminal, that is to say one with no internal intelligence. Unfortunately each time-sharing computer was independent and so the researchers could not share information with someone using a computer at another institution. That was the problem that early networking developers sought to solve.

The solution was a network called ARPANET (Advanced Research Projects Agency NETworks), which connected its first computers in 1969. The technique was called internetting because it linked together a number of independent networks of time-sharing computers. The design work for this network came long before LANs (local area networks), because the first Ethernet standard which enabled that technology did not appear until 1980. ARPANET also preceded desktop computers, which did not become commonplace until the arrival of the IBM PC in 1981.

In the late 1960s the focus was on the time-sharing of large computers and so connection was limited to 256 machines – it was inconceivable at the time that there would be the need to connect more. The arrival of LANs and PCs forced the developers to upgrade the design to accommodate the explosion of attached devices in 1983. Today the industry is moving in another new direction with a swing back towards centralised intelligence, in the form of Cloud Computing, showing again that the ultimate destination arising from a disruptive change is never certain.

ARPANET was built on top of Alexander Graham Bell's earlier disruptive change, the telephone. The original phone system carried human conversations using circuit switching and Bell never intended to use it for anything else. However, the computer network developers found that it could also carry digital messages, although not very well. During the 1960s a completely new system called packet switching was devised specifically for digital traffic and this forms the basis of all internetting. The chain of disruptions does not stop there, for in a further example of an unexpected outcome, the format which was specifically designed to handle data now carries voice traffic in a format known as VoIP (Voice over Internet Protocol). The changes in computing and communication have become more incremental over time but the concatenation of a few big disruptions continues to have a huge effect on our world.

The first killer application for networked computers was unexpected and unpredicted. Initially it was thought that the transfer of large data files would be the main use made of interconnecting computers, but in 1972 electronic mail (email) appeared. Initially this only carried the communications between the ARPANET developers, but by the turn of the century it had become a freely available product across the globe. In fact, its use has become so widespread that it has been blamed for causing the death of the hand-written letter.

The development of ARPANET was financed by the US military authorities, but its actual developers were the freer spirits of academia, so it is perhaps unsurprising that there were widely varied outcomes from the project. In 1983, the military detached its operational network as MILNET, leaving the remaining piece to grow into the internet that we know today.

There was one final hurdle that had to be jumped before the internet could really function outside its limited world. The initial system in the mid-1980s was designed and used by technicians, which meant that it needed some further work before it was ready for everyone. Tim Berners-Lee suggested that the internet should be married to hypertext in order to provide a complete solution for sharing documents across the world. The hypertext protocol is the technique for embedding control codes, or instructions within written text itself. Today these codes provide the hot links that enable navigation of both single documents and the wider universe of information. Berners-Lee had repeatedly suggested this to the relevant technical communities but when nothing happened he finally tackled the project himself and in 1991 produced the World Wide Web (WWW). To further help the process, in 1993 the NCSA (National Center for Supercomputer Applications) created Mosaic – the first popular browser which meant that all the parts were in place for the explosive growth of the internet.

The lessons that can be drawn from the disruptive change of the computing and communications industry are profound. From a few very big bangs (the telephone, creating networks that carried data, the development of email, the World Wide Web, the browser), a tidal wave of ideas, products and services have created hundreds of billions of dollars of global wealth and turned the world into an interconnected village. Clearly the full effects of this revolution are still underway, indeed one might posit that there are decades of further changes to come, albeit slower, smaller and more incremental.

Serendipity

Disruptors cannot be planned, for even the inventor of a brilliant product such as the telephone could not see the full range of outcomes. Equally some disruptors seem to have just a happy knack of happening. We will now look at some disruptive changes that have generally had positive repercussions, although in some cases they caused localised pain.

Remember to use the postcode

In the nineteenth century, letters sent to London were often delivered to the wrong address because several streets carried the same name. In 1857, Rowland Hill, the Secretary to the Post Office, removed the ambiguity by dividing the city into ten areas, EC, WC, N, E, etc., thereby creating the first post codes.

This system was refined and by 1916 the capital was subdivided further by adding a number to create more, smaller regions. Fast forward to 1959 and Ernest Marples, the Postmaster General, announced a project to create a national coding system to cover all of the UK in order to enable automatic sorting of the post. The city chosen to start things off was Norwich and 15 years and many Postmaster Generals later the scheme was completed. Although as early as 1970 everyone was exhorted to remember to use the postcode, few sorting offices were actually equipped to use them at that time. It was not until 1985 that by using OCR (Optical Character Recognition) to read envelopes directly, the automation of the whole process was finally completed. The development of postcodes, while retaining the original city codes, has however resulted in a system that has proven unsuited for bulk deliveries and so for this function a supplementary and incompatible system called Mailsort was needed. So was the 26-year project worthwhile? The answer is yes, because the story of the humble postcode does not end here.

Post coda

Although quite unforeseen by Mr Marples and the Post Office in the 1950s, the postcode has produced a number of valuable spinoffs. When the 1.5 million postcodes covering nearly 25 million addresses are linked to their map references, an accurate location of premises, typically down to a few houses within a street, is provided. Postcode information is used by internet mapping applications and GPS locators; there are databases which categorise the residents of each postcode into one of 55 distinct groups based on income, ethnicity and employment. Slicing and dicing the resulting statistics has enabled marketing companies to target their campaigns, homebuyers to evaluate neighbourhoods and the media to demonstrate the inequalities highlighted by the *postcode lottery*.

Valuable items can be postcoded, making it easier for stolen items to be recovered. Name, house number and postcode provide the fastest way for call centre staff to connect callers to their account information, and postcodes are used by insurers when setting premium levels. Home insurers use postcodes to assess the likelihood of flooding, subsidence, storm damage and burglary, and it is a similar story with car and life insurance, and annuities. In fact the postcode provides valuable services far away from its original objective to speed the journey of a letter from sender to receiver. None of this was planned, but again the initial impetus has set in motion a huge number of ideas and services.

The Blogosphere – a personal soapbox

The world of publishing has started to find the internet revolution lapping up on its shore. Earlier it was noted that email was the first killer application on the internet and that it has increasingly displaced the post (or snail mail) as a means of one-to-one communication. The rise of web logging, or blogging, has performed a similar function for one-to-many communication.

Google describes blogging as "a personal diary, a daily pulpit, a collaborative space, a political soapbox, a breaking-news outlet, a collection of links, your own private thoughts, memos to the world". Looking at this haphazard list, it is not surprising that the majority of blogs are of interest only to their authors and close family. However, in among the navel-gazers there are some serious contributors as suddenly everyone has access to a wider audience without the barrier of a publisher. One such service, Blogger, was set up in 1999 to enable non-technical people to create their own blogs and by 2010 it received around 300 million visits a month. So the nature of publishing is changing – being no longer restricted to newsprint, radio, or television, since anyone can get their opinions out there into the *blogosphere*.

Trafigura

In 2006 Trafigura, a Swiss-based multinational commodities company, sent some toxic waste to Abidjan in the Ivory Coast for processing, but instead the waste was dumped causing sickness to tens of thousands of inhabitants. In the UK, the *Guardian* newspaper became aware of a confidential report on the accident, but Trafigura's lawyers obtained an injunction preventing the paper from making the contents of the report public. Moreover, in what was dubbed a super-injunction, the newspaper was not allowed to say that it had received an injunction, nor report the involvement of Trafigura. Paul Farrelly, a British MP, asked a question in Parliament about Trafigura and so the *Guardian* asked that the injunction be relaxed to enable it to report the parliamentary event, but the lawyers refused, thereby gagging the paper from identifying the questioner, the question, the minister to whom it was addressed and where the question was to be found.

This is where blogging stepped in, initially in the guise of Twitter, the micro-blogging variant in which every posting, or tweet, is limited to a maximum of 140 characters. The *Guardian* editor, Alan

Rusbridger, tweeted "Now *Guardian* prevented from reporting parliament for unreportable reasons. Did John Wilkes live in vain?" Within 42 minutes this cryptic message had been decoded by someone quite unconnected to the *Guardian* and he posted a further tweet: "Any guesses what this is about? My money is on, ahem #TRAFIGURA!" Within a further 47 minutes a political blogger, Guido Fawkes, had posted a fuller story and pointers appeared online to the report at the centre of the storm. The next day the lawyers relaxed the injunction. A court in Amsterdam subsequently convicted the oil trader of illegally exporting waste and concealing its hazardous nature.

Trent Lott

It was a similar story in the USA. In 2002 Trent Lott, then Senate Republican Leader, was forced to resign as a direct result of the bloggings of various authors after Mr Lott made unacceptable comments on the racist policies of the Old South. The significant point in this case is that the national press and the main TV channels remained silent until a concerted attack by outraged bloggers raised the profile of the issue.

* * *

Blogging already augments traditional publishing channels by venturing into legally dangerous territory and highlighting under-reported issues, but it seems unlikely that it will replace the traditional channels of publishing and reporting altogether in its current form. At present the blogosphere is like the Wild West, offering exciting opportunities but considerable dangers to the unwary. While the mass media gives the feeling of '600 channels and nothing on', blogging can provide an alternative but because it lacks the checks and balances of the traditional media it needs to be viewed with scrutiny, for there is no authority that ensures that the blogger is competent, or even honest.

The White House in America sacked a senior black official on the basis of the contents of a blog, in which the official apparently boasted of discriminating against a white farmer 24 years previously. Later, it emerged that the blogger had deliberately edited clips in order to convey that impression. When the full record became available it showed that the official was explaining how every poor person deserved to be helped irrespective of their race. The White House was forced to offer personal and profound apologies for the pain and discomfort that had been caused to the official.

Online shopping

Another disruptive leap occurred in the creation of online shopping, which was achieved by linking communications channels to payment systems. There were around five years from the general availability of the internet until adequate security protocols and electronic payment systems were added to enable people to use it as a marketplace, but by the end of 2000 many businesses offered their services online and internet shopping has now become ubiquitous. One person who was in at the start was Jeff Bezos, a former investment banker who launched a website in 1995 to sell books over the internet. The business grew rapidly. In 1996, its first full financial year in business, it generated $15.7 million in sales and the end of 1999 saw sales reach $1.6 billion. Amazon, the company concerned, is now a multi-billion dollar business with a community of almost 40 million customers.

People everywhere now have access to the entire universe of printed books from their own homes. Search techniques enable them to find volumes from incomplete details and they are advised of related books of which they had no knowledge at all. Meanwhile, in order to survive, independent bookshops have had to emphasise the advantages that only personal shopping can provide. In 2008 Stephen Adams, owner of Kilburn Bookshop, said:

We are obviously finding it quite difficult and trading is down at the moment. Internet shopping has hit all independent bookshops for the last two or three years. It is getting worse and even bigger discounts from Amazon or the big chain stores are never good news for us.

So a technical development project undertaken originally for the military and high technology research establishments spreads its influence ever wider. Certainly the cold war leader Comrade Leonid Brezhnez, sitting in the Kremlin in 1969, would have been amazed to learn that he would, albeit indirectly, affect the fortunes of a bookseller in Highgate in 2008. The story still has far to run, for currently the development of eBooks – electronic versions of traditional print books – is changing the landscape again, so that perhaps in a few years the internet bookselling model will itself look hopelessly outdated.

Bankless banking

Frequently, disruptive changes in technology cause major disintermediation for existing players and by taking business on the internet one step further, Zopa, a UK-based company, is providing *bankless banking*. It matches lenders and borrowers directly, with both the borrowers and lenders being charged an arrangement fee by Zopa without using the savings accounts and loan applications of traditional banks.

The system matches lenders who are prepared to offer their money to potential borrowers in the format of an online auction. Matching is done on a many-to-one basis, so that each lender's loan is spread across many borrowers, thus reducing the impact of any defaults. Here the lender, effectively the depositor, has credit risk on the borrower rather than on the intermediate entity of a bank. So it is critical that the credit risk element is correctly managed to provide confidence and stability in the scheme. In the five years of operations, Zopa reports that borrower defaults have been very low.

Currently it is still a very small business in banking terms – by mid 2010 the company reported that their arranged loans had surpassed the £100 million mark and that there were over 20,000 members. It may be that by being at the low end of retail finance there is also a social aspect to the business – by offering small personal loans ranging from £10 to £25,000 to people who would find it difficult to borrow from normal sources, it could be seen as the successor to the mutual aid and social services provided by the Friendly Societies of earlier times. But with the reach provided by the internet, Zopa is not restricted to individual communities and their simple savings requirements, so it will be interesting to see if the idea migrates to other areas of finance.

Even in a country where there are a large number of individuals with no access to conventional banks, modern technology can be used to provide a service. In India, and many African countries as well, banking services are now available via the mobile phone. A consumer visits a bank correspondent at a customer service point, typically the local corner shop, supplies a password and deposits money into, or withdraws money from, his or her account. This is a high technology solution that needs no infrastructure beyond the mobile phone network which is already in place. This again demonstrates the powerful cascades of change that run through anything involving communication.

Not Quite What We Were Looking For

In the same way that disruptive changes can produce pleasant surprises, they can also produce unpleasant ones.

Bang! And British-ownership is gone

The City of London had its Big Bang in 1986. The strongly free market based ethos of the then Thatcher government was unhappy with the cosy monopoly maintained by the LSE (London Stock Exchange) in securities trading. The government felt that London was missing the opportunity to create a far bigger and potentially dominant position in the international securities market, which would match its already strong position in banking and insurance. This disruptive change involved binning the old rule books about foreign firms and restrictions on LSE membership and recognising that this meant allowing foreign groups to buy into UK stock-broking firms and participate in the London market.

At the same time two venerable but idiosyncratic ways of working were abandoned. Firstly, the distinction between jobbers (the market makers) and brokers (the client representatives) was abolished. Secondly, the privileged position of the discount houses on intermediating between the Bank of England and the money market was ended. The main objective was achieved swiftly – foreign firms flooded in, the relative position of London in international securities was strengthened and the City has subsequently gained further global market share.

On the other hand, no one foresaw the extent to which London businesses would be taken into foreign ownership. Only one of the big, old merchant banks, Rothschilds, remains under British owners. The large stock-broking firms have all gone or been absorbed into other groupings. Indeed, the financial market has seen the *Wimbledonisation* of its business – just like the famous tennis tournament, it is based in London but contested mainly by foreign players. This had not been the original intention or even the predicted outcome. Somewhat ironically some of the biggest British firms that had been staunch supporters of Mrs Thatcher's administration were blown away in the hurricane of change.

Streets ahead or a road too far?

We looked earlier at the work of Karl Benz in creating the first motorcar and developing early improvements to this vehicle. At the time, a grateful public acknowledged his work, awarding him an honorary doctorate from Karlsruhe University and a Baden State medal. Most people today would endorse those gestures because Benz created a device that makes a major contribution to their social, working and recreational lives. Of all the disruptive changes that have occurred in the past hundred years or so, most people envisage a continuation of the steady stream of supplementary incremental changes to the car that they have witnessed so far in their lives. It gives them the freedom to connect with more places and people to an extent that they cannot imagine giving up.

This freedom does come with a price though and some people, such as the social philosopher André Gorz, have opposed the car with a vehemence that would have amazed Karl Benz. In *The Social Ideology of the Motorcar* Gorz wrote:

> The worst thing about cars is that they are like castles or villas by the sea: luxury goods invented for the exclusive pleasure of a very rich minority, and which in conception and nature were never intended for the people... When everyone claims the right to drive at the privileged speed of the bourgeoisie, everything comes to a halt, and the speed of city traffic plummets... Maybe you are saying, "But at least in this way you can escape the hell of the city once the workday is over." What an impeccable circular

argument: give us more cars so that we can escape the destruction caused by cars.

Most people see the disadvantages as the price that must be paid for the benefits that come from car ownership, but the lives of children are certainly constrained by the motorcar. If children were allowed to use the streets without hindrance as they once did then even the regular journey to school would be an important play experience. Understandably parents want to protect their children from danger and traffic, even in residential streets, poses a significant threat. Unintentionally traffic engineers have contributed to this threat. They must design roads that ensure safe vehicle traffic right up to the speed limit, or risk prosecution if failure to do so causes an accident. But by concentrating on the safety of road vehicles in this way, higher traffic speeds are encouraged and the danger to pedestrians is increased. Furthermore the perception of drivers is that the street is their domain rather than that of playful children.

As traffic levels increase streets become unpleasant places to walk and are abandoned by pedestrians, both adults and children, at which time these deserted streets present a new hazard for children as there are no adults to look out for and support them. The motorcar, which at first sight seems to represent an unblemished human success story, has taken the residential street from children thereby limiting their opportunities for play and interactions with their peers. Perhaps this shortcoming, allied with others, will trigger another disruptive change in the future, sweeping the car away as quickly as it appeared. On the other hand, by further incremental improvements, its problems might be rectified and thereby ensure its survival.

It is not the objective here to predict the future, but rather to demonstrate how difficult such predictions are, even in the case of such an apparently good thing as the motorcar.

In Summary

The examples in this chapter – including the internet, the motorcar and the postcode – show that when something novel is allowed out of the laboratory, it enters a world that is so complex that the full consequences can never be known. Originators can seldom be certain of what they unleash when they instigate a disruptive change, for one change can spawn other changes and their combined effects can ripple on for decades and even centuries. Some unexpected consequences can be good, such as the communications network that was started during the cold war and now offers us unimagined shopping opportunities without leaving our homes. Some consequences can be bad, such as the loss of freedom suffered by children as a result of motor vehicles racing around our neighbourhoods.

For inventors only time will tell, for it is succeeding generations that will finally shape their creations to the needs of human society in the future. The inventors must persevere, because amongst the monsters that they unwittingly create will be the secrets for future progress. How to spot the good ideas and avoid the monsters will be explained in the next chapter.

The Futurist's Toolbag

5

Plans never survive the first engagement with the enemy.

Field Marshal Helmuth von Moltke (1800-1891)

Earlier chapters have shown how the world advances at two speeds. Firstly there is the gentle speed of incremental change and Established Practice and secondly there is the rapid speed of disruptive, or explosive change. A further important facet is that disruptive change can be triggered internally, or imposed from outside. It follows that quite different techniques are needed to handle this wide variety of challenges and it is the objective of this chapter to describe tools that can deal with each situation.

Of the hundreds of such tools which could have been chosen as illustrative examples, only the groundbreakers have been selected – those tools whose authors discovered a gap in the toolbox and produced a new solution. Today many tools are supplied for profit by companies promising a bewildering number of benefits, but without clearly explaining the precise applicability of the techniques they are offering. In this chapter the problem and the tool that can be applied to solve it are tied firmly together.

The focus is on the applicability of the tools to business, since generally it is for business that they are used. However the approaches are equally applicable right through from the individual to national government and beyond. Personal decisions that might benefit from the disciplined approaches of the tools described include choosing a new career from a range of alternatives; balancing savings against expected outgoings; or preparing for promotion or public office. Government decisions that can be helped by these tools include budget planning; reacting to the actions of other governments; and evaluating the effects of changing demographics. In fact, in any environment where a problem becomes too complex for 'flying by the seat of the pants' then the consistent approach that a tool enforces is invaluable.

Planning Not Plans

The weakness of plans based on history

Everyone makes plans every day, whether trivial or of great importance and impact, but in doing so one needs to remember one central truth; plans that are appropriate and effective where there are trends are of little or no use for events that have no precedent.

One field that illustrates this well is warfare. It has become commonplace to observe that generals usually fight the last war. Warfare rarely follows a set pattern or timeless trend, indeed change, innovation and new ideas are constantly being tried out by the military, as it is the only way to gain a significant advantage. Also the opponent is not static and is constantly seeking to do the same. In war, past experiences are never enough on which to base future plans and other techniques are needed as well.

Unsurprisingly, successful armed forces have always been interested in planning. Much effort is put into logistics, training, maintenance of equipment, discipline and proper command structures, since these are areas that can benefit from formal plans. But for strategy and reacting to the enemy, flexibility is needed in addition to advance planning. A static attitude leads to failure, for, as Wellington remarked, "All the business of war, and indeed all the business of life, is to endeavour to find out what you don't know by what you do; that's what I called 'guessing what was at the other side of the hill.' "

As in war, so it is in other spheres and history is full people who erroneously believed that past experience was enough to predict the future. From Alexander Graham Bell, who said in 1924 "...the day would come when the man at the telephone would be able to see the distant person to whom he was speaking", to Dick Tracy who since 1964 has sported a two-way wrist TV, people have predicted that the video-phone will be the next big thing in telecommunications. But its arrival has been very slow, meanwhile text messaging, a less glamorous (perhaps even retrograde) development, has exploded. There were estimated to be 2.4 billion active texters worldwide by 2007 with academic studies concluding that usage was addictive.

Here are some famous quotes by other people who thought that they could see the future:

Inventions reached their limit long ago and I see no hope of further development.

Julius Sextus Frontinus, Roman engineer, 35-103AD

It is only a toy.

President of Western Union on being offered the patent for the telephone by Alexander Graham Bell, 1876

Computers in the future may weigh no more than 1.5 tons.

Popular Mechanics Magazine, 1949

We don't like their sound, and guitar music is on the way out.

Decca Recording Company on The Beatles, 1962

The Five-Year Plans of the State Planning Committee of the Soviet Union (GOSPLAN) represent the most extreme example in recent times of trying to predict the future and making plans from that prediction. The Soviet government believed that a centrally planned economy could be made to serve political and economic objectives for the long-term common good and they further believed that central planning ensured optimal use of all resources, both material and human.

However, they discovered that meaningful five-year planning was impossible. The complexity of the problem meant that they were forced to make gross simplifications, so that they could not accurately allocate goods and services. Crucially there was no way to anticipate new inventions or efficiency improvements and include them in the prediction. Consequently local managers had no incentive to incorporate anything new that arrived during the execution of a five-year plan, since making a change would be risky and even if it were successful, they would get no credit.

Tell me a story

This does not mean that one should admit defeat and do nothing to prepare for the future, but rather it should be recognised that simple plans, or more precisely plans with a single outcome, are not enough. The human race has always faced this dilemma and has always needed a solution to ensure survival. The first solution was based upon language and picturing the future through stories. At first such stories would have been used to warn of dangers, but over time they were expanded to establish laws and customs, resolve conflicts and record history.

The universality of this approach can be gauged by the fact that every culture has had a name for the teller of such stories. This would have been a soothsayer in Roman times; a jester, minstrel, or storyteller in Medieval Europe; brehon, bard, seanachaidhean in Celtic lands; Kathakars in India; Griot in Africa, and so on. The Indian epic, the Mahabharata, stresses its own importance with the words, "If you listen carefully, at the end you'll be someone else." In Mande, West Africa, the tradition has survived to the present. There the Jeli is an historian and advisor through whom the king communicates to others. He accompanies the king at all times and commits to memory every notable event including battles. A Jeli passes his memories to his heir to preserve the stories down the generations. This way a collective memory is built up and crucially can be drawn upon to offer ideas, advice and guidance for the future. Quite simply, storytelling is a key method for passing on knowledge, which every culture uses.

Memories of the future

Approaching the same truth from a different direction, the late Professor David Ingvar, a Swedish neurobiologist, examined the scientific basis for storytelling. He found that a specific area of the brain, the frontal/prefrontal cortex, handles behaviour and knowledge along a timeline and it also handles action plans for future behaviour. Ingvar's research demonstrated that damage in that area of the brain results in an inability to foresee the consequences of one's future behaviour. He concluded that the brain is hardwired to do this and that plans are created instinctively every moment of our lives; planning for the immediate future, that day, that week and even years ahead. As these plans can be retained and recalled, Ingvar called them "memories of the future".

This can be illustrated with a simple example. When someone takes up a new interest or sport, say skiing, that person notices lots of magazine articles, perhaps special sales offers on ski equipment, and more and more people talking about skiing. This media focus on skiing was not noticed before, is it a coincidence or is something weird going on? In fact it's neither, for, as Ingvar's research demonstrated, the new skier is now turning his or her mind to potential future pathways and outcomes – in this case skiing – and as a result is building a memory of the future that centres around planned skiing trips and adventures.

This activity is crucial, for if the mind is not opened to such pathways and planning, information on a given topic is not retained. The brain is continually bombarded with a vast number of unordered stimuli such as sights, sounds and smells which cannot all be assimilated and so there must be a high level of filtering. All the input the brain receives is compared with previously constructed future memories and if there is no match it is discarded. In other words, an unforeseen event cannot be seen at all and goes straight over your head, or perhaps more literally does not stick in the brain. Most dramatically this occurs with close up

> **"** At the group or corporate level where there is more than one brain involved, it is far harder to create a shared library of memories of the future. **"**

conjurors and other illusionists, but it occurs in everyday life where a change can be unrecognised until long after any practical reaction can be taken – for example the Wimbledonisation of the City of London; the move of the computer onto the desk; the worldwide distribution of music.

At the group or corporate level where there is more than one brain involved, it is far harder to create a shared library of memories of the future. However, the importance of rehearsing all likely possible futures is clearly an important tool and this was recognised in the 1980s by Royal/Dutch Shell who use it as the technical basis for their planning technique of scenarios, as will be discussed later in this chapter.

In Chapter 1 we recounted the story of the Rainhill trials for the selection of the locomotive for the Liverpool & Manchester railway and there is a coda to this story that fits in with Ingvar's research. At the opening ceremony of the railway, which was the first in the world to have double tracks, the local Liverpool MP and former Cabinet Minister William Huskisson was killed by one of the locomotives as he left his carriage and was unaware of another train coming in the opposite direction. He had no previous thoughts or memories of how railways would operate, and so he was unprepared for the risks posed by two tracks and multiple engines.

Whether Forecast?

Future planning can be ranked by the desirability or likelihood of outcomes. Not all new developments or innovation projects are the same and consequently not all methodologies are appropriate. A UK government paper, 'A Futurist's Toolbox; Methodologies in Futures Work' (2001) suggests categorisation by the three Ps; probable, possible and preferable. These can be defined as follows:

- *Probable future*: what is most likely to happen. Predicting the future by statistical extrapolations from the current situation.

- *Possible futures*: what may happen. This involves foresight, as opposed to forecasting, where there is insufficient evidence to predict a single outcome and a range of possible futures must be identified.

- *Preferable future*: where the future can be controlled. This can also be termed making the weather, where it is possible to obtain a desired outcome by one's own actions.

From this simple categorisation some basic observations can be made.

It is easier to plan for a *probable future* than to set out the multiple alternatives of several *possible futures*, but to depend on a future that never comes can be a disaster. For example, property developers might see overcrowded offices and conclude that more offices will be needed in the future. Anticipating this probable outcome they buy land, obtain planning permission, and build and equip offices, only to find that in the intervening years there has been a great increase in home working and the offices are not wanted. If they had looked at a number of possible developments in working patterns and kept their options open, they might have avoided this pitfall. Keeping one's options open can be expensive, in both money and time. On a personal basis, prior to buying a house, one might pay for surveys on several properties and thereby incur extra expenditure, but this precaution ensures that the final choice is based upon the fullest possible information and the chance of making an expensive mistake is reduced.

Working towards a *preferred future* – following a process that is popularly called a *roadmap* – is a luxury that is only open to the very largest organisations and (counter-intuitively) to start up entrepreneurs. The process is most easily understood through some examples. The government might work towards a preferred future where no one smokes. To reduce support costs, a large software developer might work towards a preferred future where everyone upgrades to the latest operating system. An entrepreneur might invent something that no one has considered and so for which there can be no demand until it is launched, at which point it creates the future.

The futurist tools that are described in the rest of this chapter are divided according to their suitability within these three broad categories, namely probable, possible and preferable futures. Within these overall headings they are divided further depending on whether the facts are quantitative, hard to find, or hard to connect; and whether a large company or entrepreneur is involved. To show clearly which tools are best suited to which problem, they are linked into a flow diagram in Figure 5.1.

Figure 5.1 – Selecting the right tool for the job

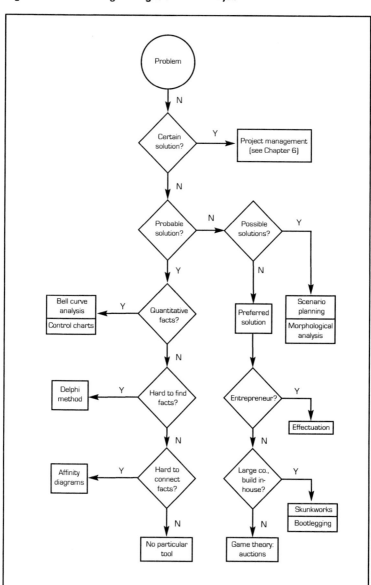

Predicting The Future

A single prediction for the future can and should be used whenever there is sufficient historical evidence. For example, discounted cash flow, market research and sales analysis can be used to predict the development of a mature company. Where the evidence consists of numerical data that is dependent on random variables, the appropriate statistical tool is *bell curve analysis*. One example is actuarial data, which gives a sound basis for life insurance products, and another is the historical data that is used to price options and other financial derivatives.

In manufacturing, measurement and statistical analysis can be used to ensure future production quality, using such a tool as *the control chart*. This measures trends using time series and extrapolations or other statistical analyses in order to reach a unique solution. Where the history consists of a mixture of numbers, non-numeric facts and opinions, then extracting the single probable future is harder, but methodologies have been developed to guide the process. For example *the Delphi method* works on the principle that many heads are better than one and the *affinity diagram* simplifies problems by organising the facts into groups that can be more easily understood and dealt with.

In the following sub-sections these tools are described in more detail.

Bell curve analysis

The bell curve (see Figure 5.2) that results from a normal distribution can be used to describe any facts which cluster around a mean (usually denoted as μ), such as the heights of men in a population. More data points lie around the mean value (at the top of the bell) than any other value, but there are data points at values some distance away from the mean (at the sides of the bell). The frequency of occurrences falls away symmetrically on either side of the mean until occurrences are most unlikely. The rate at which values fall away, the fatness of the bell, is given by the standard deviation, which is usually denoted by the Greek symbol sigma (σ).

Figure 5.2 – The normal distribution bell curve

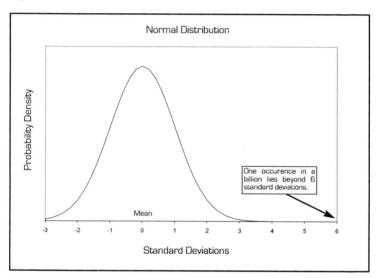

The normal distribution was named by Karl Pearson, founder of the first university statistics department at University College London in 1911, and incidentally student and biographer of Sir Francis Galton. He called it *normal* because it applies in a surprisingly wide set of circumstances, even when the underlying facts are determined by random variables which are themselves not normally distributed.

The simplest illustration is the repeated tossing of a coin. Each toss is random, but certainly not normally distributed since the only possible outcomes are heads (0, say), or tails (1, say). If the coin is tossed 1000 times, the most likely total score, the mean, is 500, but any score near to 500 is likely and a score a long way from 500 is possible. If the experiment is repeated a very large number of times, then the frequency of particular scores will take up the familiar bell shape. So individual random events that are themselves not normally distributed, when they are summed, construct the familiar bell shape of outcomes. Taking a more sophisticated example, suppose that complex inherited factors combine with some external factors such as diet to determine the heights of men in a population. Unlike the simple coin tossing, the distribution of each factor is unknown, but it is unlikely to be normal. Nevertheless, the resulting distribution of heights is likely to be roughly normal.

The great attraction of assuming a normal distribution when predicting the future is that the mass of data is completely described by just two variables – the mean and the likely distance from the mean (the standard deviation). Simple rules of thumb indicate the likelihood of a value occurring away from the mean; there is a **" The power of such simple rules as those of the normal distribution brings danger if too much is read into the results. "** 32% chance of an event being more than one standard deviation away from the mean, a 5% chance of it being more than two standard deviations and a 0.3% chance of the event being more than three standard deviations from the mean. Any event that occurs much beyond three standard deviations can generally be interpreted as a warning that the distribution is no longer normal. Any event outside six standard deviations is almost certainly not normal, since that theory would indicate that it is a one-in-half-a-billion occurrence.

The power of such simple rules as those of the normal distribution brings danger if too much is read into the results. When designing car seats, the dimensions should not be based on the heights of a handful of men. More subtly, difficulties might emerge if two distinct groups are merged. For instance, taking the heights of a mixture of men and women does not give a single bell curve but a curve with two humps, one around the average height for a woman and one around the average height for a man. This is because two groups cannot be lumped together whose heights are determined by two different sets of random variables and there must be two sets, since the average man is taller than the average woman. It worked for men only, because although the precise workings of the factors were not understood, every member had the same bunch of factors, but by combining the two sexes that rule was violated. Clearly the assumption of normality should be made with care. As Pearson himself said:

> I can only recognise the occurrence of the normal curve – the Laplacian curve of errors – as a very abnormal phenomenon. It is roughly approximated to in certain distributions; for this reason, and on account of its beautiful simplicity, we may, perhaps, use it as a first approximation, particularly in theoretical investigations.

Not everyone is as cautious as Karl Pearson for the normal distribution is now embedded in the calculations for the values of most financial derivatives. Of these, probably the best known is the Black-Scholes calculator for equity options, which is based on changes in the logarithm of the prices of the underlying equity.

The control chart

In the 1920s Western Electric used amplifiers that were buried in the ground in order to boost telephone signals and because of their location they were expensive to replace. The company needed a way of knowing when the production quality of amplifiers was worsening – and thus when the manufacturing process was in need of correction – before faulty amplifiers went into the field. This was a very short-term forecasting requirement compared with most of the others described in this book, but in its own way it was as vital to the continued success of Western Electric as the more momentous choices made from time to time.

Engineering inspector Walter Shewhart produced a single page memo describing the problem and its solution in the form of what came to be called the control chart, plotting measurements from samples taken at regular time intervals. Even when all was well, these measurements would not be identical, but would vary in some non-assignable way, which Shewhart called the *common-cause variation*.

If all was not well and problems were arising that needed attention, then there would be an additional variation that could be assigned to a specific cause. This he called the *special-cause variation*. A standardised control chart separated the two effects and enabled the operator to see the point at which the machine should be stopped and adjusted to avoid producing faulty amplifiers. As this was a statistical solution, sometimes the machine would be stopped unnecessarily and sometimes the machine would be allowed to run after it should have been stopped for adjustment, but overall amplifiers were produced with minimum corrections of the machine and few needed to be withdrawn after deployment.

Shewhart's work came to the attention of W. Edwards Deming, an engineer from Iowa, who became its foremost champion, but in the immediate post-war years he found few takers in the USA, where there was unprecedented demand for goods and so the emphasis was on quantity rather than quality. The situation in Japan was quite different as it struggled to convert its shattered industrial base back to full production. During General MacArthur's rule in the immediate period after the war, the US government provided help with this process in the form of professional advisors. Deming was part of the advisory team and he found a much more receptive audience for the control chart concept and other aspects of quality management in Japan than back home. Positive results were soon achieved, ironically at the expense of American industry. Deming was feted in Japan, where the Japanese Union of Scientists and Engineers established the Deming Prize in his honour, the emperor awarded him the Second Order Medal of the Sacred Treasure and Toyota placed his photograph in the entrance hall of their Head Office.

The enthusiasm of the Japanese for the control chart is easily understood because it ensured products of a higher quality. When Ford produced a car with transmissions made in both the USA and Japan, their US customers demanded the Japanese version because of its superior build quality even though they had to wait longer for delivery.

> " Six Sigma improves the quality of existing products and services through close attention to statistical detail, but it does not help nurture new products or disruptive techniques. "

Unfortunately American industry took a long time to learn the lesson, for although Deming had returned to the USA, he was largely ignored, and continued to work in relative obscurity until in 1980 he was featured in an NBC documentary entitled 'If Japan can... Why Can't We?' This renewed publicity late in life, at a time when US public opinion was increasingly fearful of the Japanese takeover of US industry, meant that he was engaged in a new stream of consulting projects up until his death in 1993 aged 93.

At last the cycle had turned and US businesses had recognised the importance of giving value to the customer. With renewed vigour and belief they took the ideas that they had previously rejected and re-invented them as Six Sigma, the quality system adopted by Motorola and popularised by Jack Welch of General Electric. The name Six Sigma is curious and somewhat contentious. It is derived from the standard deviation, σ, of bell curve analysis, but Six Sigma is taken to represent 3.4 defects per million, rather than the 2 defects per billion that the mathematics would suggest.

To a statistician the technique should be called four and a half sigma, but that does not roll off the tongue so neatly. A more serious accusation levelled at the technique is that if it is employed indiscriminately across an organisation it can stifle invention. It is a technique to refine Established Practice through incremental change. That is to say that Six Sigma improves the quality of existing products and services through close attention to statistical detail, but it does not help nurture new products or disruptive techniques. If it is applied relentlessly, so that regimes that are suited to disruptive change are pushed out, then innovation is stifled. This was the experience of 3M, whose new CEO James McNerney, in 2000, instituted a Six Sigma program which brought discipline to an unwieldy, erratic and sluggish company, at the expense of the innovative culture that had made it. Art Fry, a long-time employee and inventor of the Post-it note, concluded that "there was no way in the world that anything like a Post-it note would emerge from this new system". As will be seen later in the chapter, inventors and inventions need a quite different regime.

The Delphi method

The Delphi method is not well named, for it is quite unconnected to the ravings of the sibyl in ancient Greece. Rather it is a technique used to obtain the most probable future from inputs from all of the relevant experts. The basis of this approach is alluded to in such common sayings as 'Two heads are better than one' and 'Let's put our heads together over this'. The first person to investigate formally whether these sayings were valid was Sir Francis Galton. He examined the tickets in a 'Guess the weight' competition at an agricultural fair and his analysis was as follows:

> In these democratic days [universal suffrage was a topic of interest at the time], any investigation into the trustworthiness and peculiarities of popular judgement is of interest... A weight-judging competition was carried on

at the West of England Fat Stock and Poultry Exhibition recently held at Plymouth... It appears then, in this particular instance, that the *vox populi* is correct within 1% of the real value... This result is, I think, more reliable than might have been expected.

Nature, **7 March, 1907**

In 1946, at the beginning of the cold war, the Douglas Aircraft Company in California started Project RAND to study "the broad subject of intercontinental warfare, other than surface". It found that traditional forecasting methods were not appropriate when there were no supporting scientific laws, or when accurate information was unavailable or expensive to obtain. From these initial observations the Delphi method was developed by Olaf Helmer, Norman Dalkey and Nicholas Rescher to fill that gap. Like Galton, RAND gathered together all of the relevant experts, although this time they were military men rather than pig farmers.

Delphi provides a consistent group communication process for the experts from which the most reliable consensus of opinion can be drawn. Through anonymity it solves the usual problems of group dynamics and ensures that every expert that should be heard is heard, that opinions are freely given and that where appropriate opinions are changed in response to feedback. The first study undertaken was the application of "expert opinion to the selection, from the point of view of a Soviet strategic planner, of an optimal US industrial target system and to the estimation of the number of A-bombs required to reduce the munitions output by a prescribed amount". Given the sensitive nature of that first exercise, it is not surprising that the technique did not emerge from the defence community immediately.

It was 1964 before the method did become publicly known, and it has since been used throughout the world on a wide range of long-term planning topics including the impacts of scientific breakthroughs, population control, automation, space exploration, war prevention, weapons systems, environment, health and transportation. It can and has been used anywhere that work must be done and money spent, before the justification can be provided using traditional methods. Over the years, the Delphi method has been challenged and improvements suggested, but it remains the basis for much forecasting work today.

Affinity diagrams

A natural way to tackle a complex issue is through brainstorming, where everyone involved offers every idea that they have on the subject without any restraints. The result is often a very large number of unordered and sometimes overlapping ideas. Affinity diagrams provide a technique by which these unstructured thoughts can be condensed into a manageable number of overarching themes. The technique emerged, as so did many of these tools, as a spin-off from someone who had a real problem to solve and who found that at the time there were no suitable methods available.

That person was Jiro Kawakita who was born in Tokyo in 1920 and studied geography at university. In 1953 he joined the Japan Alpine Club on a major expedition to the Sikha vally, on the south-western slopes of the mountain Annapurna 1 in Nepal. There he studied the region's plant ecology and developed a lifetime attachment to Nepal, calling it "this beloved land". Kawakita organised further trips to the region where his research suggested that the Sikha Valley "was experiencing an ecological disaster of major proportions". Population growth over the previous century had upset the balance of humans, cattle, forage, food and firewood.

He found that standard anthropological field techniques were inadequate to analyse such practical situations. While it was possible to study separately the environment, population, kinship, village organisation and religious belief, it missed their crucial interrelationships. His solution, which became known as the KJ Method, or affinity diagrams, enabled him to draw conclusions from chaotic inputs. Kawakita wrote each item of data on an individual label, and then grouped the labels by their perceived relationships. Each group was named and the process continued by grouping the groups until a manageable number of super-groups emerged.

For the villages of the Sikha valley, Kawakita concluded that the basic needs of the villagers could be met by two relatively low-tech innovations. Ropelines were needed for the transport of animal fodder, firewood and manure down the mountainside, and pipelines were needed to bring clean water into the villages. Appropriately, a decision-making tool which emphasises the linking of factors found solutions which proposed physical links. Kawakita recognised that the methods that he had pioneered in Nepal had a much wider applicability. From this initial experience he founded the Kawakita Research Institute in Tokyo and used this to disseminate the KJ Method.

Kawakita had found the standard techniques inadequate, and for him the major challenge was the inter-relationships of the fundamental data. The people at the RAND Corporation also found standard techniques inadequate, but for them the major challenge was getting the fundamental data. Subsequent critics of the Delphi method regard the lack of cross correlation between questions as a weakness and so perhaps an amalgamation of the two techniques might be superior to either one alone.

Foresight Not Forecast

The tools described so far are designed to seek out the single most probable outcome. For situations where this is not practical, it is important to recognise the fact and not try to simplify matters by selecting an arbitrary outcome. IBM thought that they were only getting into the home computer market when they produced the first PC. Jan Winston worked on the original project and admits that they did not fully understand what was happening. He said "the broad acceptance of the computer, the way it embedded itself in our everyday lives and the explosion of the internet, is an order of magnitude beyond what we were thinking about in the early 1980s." The company simply did not anticipate the effect the personal computer would have on other IBM ranges. As we saw in Chapter 3, problems which are ill-defined and for which no single solution exists, are called messes. In such circumstances the best that can be done is to identify a number of possible futures and be ready to deal with whichever one arrives. The classic technique for this situation is scenario planning, while a second, more mechanised, tool is morphological analysis (MA).

Scenario planning

The importance of storytelling for the individual has already been described along with Ingvar's suggestion that the facility is hardwired into our brain as part of our evolutionary survival kit. Scenario planning can be thought of as giving an organisation a storytelling capability, by enabling it to create, develop and maintain *memories of the future*.

A strange love of the possible

An early pioneer of scenario planning was Herman Kahn, on whom the fictional Dr Strangelove, portrayed by Peter Sellers, was partially based. Kahn began his career in the late 1940s with the RAND Corporation and, possessing an incredibly high IQ, he rose to be co-director of the Strategic Air Force Project. His main concern was that the USA of the early 1960s had a false picture of the likelihood and effects of nuclear war. The existing doctrine was based upon a balance of power where the two sides, the USA and Russia, could press a button and annihilate the other side, thus creating a situation of mutually assured destruction. Kahn concluded that since nuclear weapons effectively cancelled each other out, the real threat came from conventional arms and there, Russia was superior. He published these ideas in *On Thermonuclear War* in 1960.

Kahn's method was to think about the unthinkable and to look for acceptable alternatives, and his work had a major impact on US military thinking at the time. In 1961 he founded the Hudson Institute, initially a defence-oriented think tank, but by the late 1960s it had expanded into the study of a broad range of social policy issues, from which *futurology* emerged. In 1967 Kahn wrote *The Year 2000* with Anthony J. Weiner, which set out the principles of scenario planning, a term coined by Kahn and taken from the film industry where it means a sketch of the plot of a play that gives particulars of the scenes, situations, etc.

Kahn defined *scenarios* as attempts to describe in some detail a hypothetical sequence of events that could plausibly lead to the situation envisaged. The objective of scenarios was to dramatise a larger range of possibilities, thereby calling attention to principles, issues or questions that might otherwise be ignored. Some people thought that scenarios could be so divorced from reality as to be dangerous, but Kahn and Weiner rejected that view:

> Since plausibility is a great virtue in a scenario, one should, subject to other considerations, try to achieve it. But it is important not to limit oneself to the most plausible, conventional or probable situations and behaviour. History is likely to write scenarios that most observers would find implausible not only prospectively but sometimes, even, in

retrospect. Many sequences of events seem plausible now only because they have actually occurred; a man who knew no history might not believe any. Future events may not be drawn from the restricted list of those we have learned are possible; we should expect to go on being surprised.

Scenario planning and the private sector

The company that took scenario planning into the private sector was Royal Dutch Shell. For conventional business development they had launched the Unified Planning Machinery in 1967, which was supposed to be the "planning system to end all planning systems". The procedures were set out in a thick manual, which all managers had to follow. The culmination of the process was an annual presentation to the Committee of Managing Directors. Unfortunately, in the words of Arie de Geus, a key planner at Shell, "whenever times are turbulent, and anticipating the future is most critical, the Unified Planning Machinery is wrong. Dead wrong."

One year later, a new planning division was created at the company under Pierre Wack, which built on Kahn's ideas to create Shell's own form of the scenario technique. The scenario planners did not restrict themselves to narrow oil industry concerns, but included what was changing in a wide variety of arenas: social values, technology, consumption patterns, political thinking and international finance.

In one scenario, an accident in Saudi Arabia led to the severing of an oil pipeline, decreasing supply and raising prices enabling the OPEC nations to pump less oil and make more money. The executives considered the implications of this scenario so that when OPEC announced its first oil embargo, which was equivalent to a fractured pipe, Shell could handle the challenges better and faster than the opposition.

In 1983, Wack's successor, Peter Schwartz, undertook a study of the future of the Soviet Union, the possessor of some of the largest oil and gas reserves in the world. At that time, these reserves had little effect on Shell, because for political reasons Europe had made an informal agreement that no more than 35% of its markets would be available to the Soviet Union. Furthermore, with Reagan and Thatcher on one side and Andropov on the other there was no likelihood that the Soviet Union would invite foreign firms to participate in their oil industry. Nevertheless, Schwartz and his colleagues created a scenario to investigate the implications of such an eventuality. With the arrival of Mikhail Gorbachev and perestroika in 1985-6 this unlikely but possible event occurred. Through their foresight, Shell was prepared. They cut costs on the expensive Troll gas fields and delayed buying oil fields until the price of oil had fallen from $30 to $15 per barrel.

> " The objective of scenarios is to dramatise a larger range of possibilities, thereby calling attention to principles, issues or questions that might otherwise be ignored. "

Since being popularised by Shell, scenario planning has become a standard tool in many industries besides government and the military, where it is used to help organisations prepare for the possible rather than just the probable. The technique has been developed and refined over the years and is considered by many planners as vital in helping to understand future uncertainties, to rehearse responses and, when they spot a particular scenario unfold, to react swiftly.

Morphological analysis

Originally the science of *morphology* was concerned with the geometrical shape of things and with the changes of these shapes with time; in that sense Goethe occupied himself with the morphology of plants. Fritz Zwicky, an astrophysicist based at the California Institute of Technology, took the word and generalised it to embrace the investigation not merely of geometrical patterns but of characteristics of all things and particularly how they are built by connecting components. As such, the morphological method is nothing more than an orderly way of looking at things. Zwicky pointed out that unconsciously scientists had been already employing morphological thinking. He said:

A brilliant example of the power of the morphological procedure may be found in the scientific achievements of Faraday, from whom its essential features become apparent. It is the interrelation between the coexisting aspects of nature which is stressed. Thus Faraday, instead of investigating this or that physical effect, was interested primarily in correlations among all phenomena. In visualising the various fields of physics, that is, geometry, kinematics and dynamics, he asked for bonds between them and set out to explore them systematically. Faraday's successes along this line of thought are well known. For instance, his law of induction established the triple relation among electricity, magnetism and mechanical motion.

The trigger for the conscious use of morphology was, as with so many futurist tools, the Second World War, and its first application was in the field of propulsive power plants. The morphological analysis of jet engines was carried out theoretically and the results were translated into the construction and operation of a series of these engines.

As with Jiro Kawakita, Zwicky had to develop a tool in order to solve the particular problem at hand. Zwicky recognised that the techniques had applicability outside the world of pure science, but he cautioned that in wider society and statecraft (areas where morphological analysis could be most beneficial) "prejudices, conventions and narrow ideologies interfere" to make the application of morphological analysis more difficult.

Also like Jiro Kawakita, Zwicky believed that the *connections* between facts and ideas were of paramount importance and this led him to complain about conventional education in tones that were similar to those of Peter Hyman that we saw in Chapter 2.

He said:

Morphological thinking suggests that this new approach cannot be realised through increased teaching of specialised knowledge.

Although Zwicky continued to advance the morphological approach until his death in 1974, its method of execution mitigated against its adoption at that time. In its nature of stressing the importance of investigating *every* connection, even the unlikely ones, it threw up enormous numbers of alternatives. This meant that its general application was not possible in Zwicky's lifetime, but had to await cheap and accessible computers to take the drudgery out of the task.

The baton was taken up in the early 1990s by the Swedish Defence Research Agency. They produced a computer-based tool, MA/Casper. This turned the inherent disadvantage of morphological analysis into an advantage, since not only did it automate the process, it provided an audit trail so that investigators could see why a path had been selected and a *what-if* facility so that perturbations could be examined.

Like Delphi, MA/Casper combines the inputs from a panel of experts. The lack of general availability of this tool has restricted its wider use, nevertheless it has been employed on more than 80 non-quantifiable questions such as 'What are we going to do with the Swedish bomb shelter programme, now that the cold war is over?' This particular question illustrates the flexibility of morphological analysis, containing as it does financial, technical, political, geographical and ethical dimensions, with both quantifiable and non-quantifiable variables.

Making The Weather

Under some circumstances powerful organisations such as governments and large corporations do not have to wait to see *what turns up*, because they can make their preferred future happen. Counter-intuitively, visionary entrepreneurs – which in business terms are the exact opposite of large organisations – can do so too. In neither case is success guaranteed.

Governments and large organisations are structured in ways that are unsuitable for creating a future that does not look like the past and so sometimes it is necessary for them to remove some controls in order to allow creativity to flourish. This can be done by setting up a parasite organisation which has looser controls. Alternatively, staff can be encouraged to follow their own ideas alongside their formal tasks and hope that something turns up. These approaches are respectively called *skunkworks* and *bootlegging*.

Entrepreneurs have to work backwards, starting with what they have and creating the market and alliances needed, rather than using the conventional process of investigating the market needs and building products to satisfy them. This is *effectuation* and the process was explained by one entrepreneur as 'Fire, Ready, Aim'!

When an organisation has something which it wishes to sell, but is unsure of its precise value, it can let the purchasers provide the valuation through sale by auction. This is well understood in the world of antiques and fine art, but more recently the concept has been incorporated into the science of *game theory* and auctions have been used by governments to sell telecommunication frequency spectra. It is hard to imagine anything further removed from the traditional auction house.

We will now look at skunkworks, bootlegging, effectuation and game theory in turn.

Skunkworks

An onerous and odorous task

Skunkworks developed as a method for dealing with an apparently intractable problem during, once again, the Second World War. In 1943, Allied intelligence reports revealed that Germany was developing a new high-speed fighter, powered by a propellerless 'jet'. This was no time to sift alternatives and predict possible or probable outcomes – with preparations for the D-Day invasion of France already in hand the Allies needed a new aeroplane to match the German threat in the ridiculously short time frame of six months. They turned to the Lockheed Aircraft Corporation who set up an Advanced Development Projects Unit under Kelly Johnson. This was a somewhat grandiose title for a team of fifty occupying a rented circus tent in Burbank, California. The tent was next to a plastics factory and the smell was such that one of the engineers began answering the phone "Skonk works…" after the illicit still that produced kickapoo juice in the *L'il Abner* comic strip. From this the term *skunkworks* was born.

To give some perspective on the time frame, in 2002 Boeing set the objectives for a new airliner, the 787 Dreamliner, and the aircraft made its first international trip in 2010, almost 3000 days later. By comparison, Johnson's team of 23 design engineers and 30 shop mechanics delivered the first prototype P-80 Shooting Star in 143 days. In fact the war ended before the plane, could be deployed and it did not see active service until the Korean War. Nevertheless, the Lockheed skunkworks had demonstrated that a small focussed team could deliver a result that was not remotely possible by normal development and production methods. The good results continued with innovative fighting aircraft such as the F-104, U2 and SR-71. Success was not guaranteed however and sometimes the corner cutting produced "absolute clunkers", according to insider Ben Rich.

Kelly Johnson ran the skunkworks unit at Burbank until 1966 under the motto "Be quick, be quiet, be on time", which he backed up with 14 further rules. The most important of these rules for general use are: "the Skunk Works manager must be delegated practically complete control of his program in all aspects" and "use a small number of good people (10% to 25%) compared to the so-called normal systems." Further requirements were that no report to Johnson should be longer than 20 pages and that no meeting should have more than 15 attendees.

This idea has been taken up by many organisations, particularly by those which have urgently needed to react to a threat or an opportunity by moving to a higher speed of progress. In general, a skunkworks project operates with the general approval of management, but without the detailed reporting and bureaucracy that is required for normal work. Such projects are usually concerned with advanced concepts and are undertaken in secret. If the development is successful then the resultant product is moved out of the skunkworks and made subject to standard corporate processes.

> " To build something with no discernible market is the sort of thing that a start-up entrepreneur can try. "

The IBM PC – the upside and downside of skunkworks

In the mid-1970s computers became available for home use, despite the incredulity expressed by Ken Olsen of DEC. The early ones were based on chips designed to control traffic signals and were delivered to enthusiasts in kit form. A major step was the production of the MITS Altair 8800 in 1975, which the suppliers claimed to be as powerful as a mini-computer and it was publicised on the cover of *Popular Electronics*. MITS's Ed Roberts was gambling that enough of the 450,000 readers would pay $400 to build a computer even if they did not have the slightest idea how to use it. To build something with no discernible market is the sort of thing that a start-up entrepreneur like Roberts can try, as is described later in this chapter. Large corporations frequently find it difficult to be as flexible and open to new ideas.

It was certainly not easy for a huge company like IBM to deal with the challenges these developments created. They were looking with some concern at a burgeoning home computer market, which by 1979 was a multi-million dollar business. Their first attempt in the small business computer space had been the IBM 5100 that cost between $10,000 and $20,000 and weighed 50 pounds. An analyst at the time commented that "IBM bringing out a personal computer would be like teaching an elephant to tap dance". Another said "it would take IBM a year just to design an empty box". What they needed was a team that could skirt the bureaucracy. What they needed was a skunkworks.

The Entry Level Systems IBU (Independent Business Unit) made a proposal to IBM top management that they would build a machine for this market place in 18 months, an unbelievably short time for that organisation and its existing business methods. The proposal was accepted and a team of 12 started in Boca Raton, Florida, in an old, uncomfortable warehouse. Sure enough, 18 months later in August 1981 the PC was launched at a price of $1565. In one move IBM had moved an industry for hobbyists into the mainstream and success was immediate.

By 1985, the division had 10,000 employees, one million units had been sold and revenues of $4.5 billion generated. Before the PC, the best-selling IBM computer is said to have sold 25,000 units. Lou Gerstner, who had become CEO in 1993, had a dig at the sceptical analyst mentioned earlier when he entitled the memoirs of his time at IBM *Who Says Elephants Can't Dance?* However, as a caveat to this success, the corner which the skunkworks team cut in order to achieve their targets (namely the decision to outsource almost everything) contained the seeds of ultimate failure and demonstrates that sometimes red tape has a purpose.

Traditionally IBM was organised vertically, making its own hardware, writing its own software and selling directly to customers. To meet the timescales the skunkworks team delegated the processor to Intel, the operating system to Microsoft and the selling of the machines to consumer electronic stores and Sears Roebuck. They believed that despite all of this outsourcing they could keep control of the product through ownership of a key piece of logic, the Basic Input/Output System (BIOS), which acts as a gateway through which all data must pass.

Unfortunately, competitors cloned the BIOS without actually stealing code from IBM and the PC Compatible was born. This was of course a great disadvantage to IBM, but to the benefit of the rest of the world, most especially Microsoft. Meanwhile with no control over the monster it had produced, PCs were linked together to form networks, which fatally undermined IBM's core mainframe computer business. The IBM PC story illustrates both the strength and the weakness of the skunkworks.

Bootlegging

A skunkworks is set up by management with a definite objective, but then is not run under the tight controls that are applied to mainstream projects. Bootlegging offers a further degree of freedom, in that it does not even have an overall management objective.

Scotch Tape

In 1925 Richard Drew joined the 3M Company and his first job was in a car body paint shop testing their new sandpaper, then the only product that the company made. While there he noticed that the painters were having problems where two colours met. The plaster tape that they used as a guide either damaged the paint or could not be removed at all. He experimented for a couple of weeks to produce an alternative, but was then told to get back to testing the sandpaper. Ignoring the management command, he persevered and developed a prototype of a non-drying adhesive tape. The sample that he took to the painters had insufficient adhesive and so they said "Take this tape back to those Scotch (i.e. mean) bosses of yours and tell them to put more adhesive on it!" More adhesive was added and the new version of the tape worked, so that both a new product and its name were born.

The success of the masking tape caused 3M management to think about how new products were developed. They concluded that they could arise anywhere, but particularly from the people in the front line, even though they may be junior and inexperienced staff. So 3M implemented a revolutionary policy called the 15%-time rule. Under this rule, regardless of their assignments, 3M technical employees were encouraged to devote 15% of their working hours to independent projects.

The best known product that has emerged from the scheme is the Post-it note. Spencer Silver accidentally discovered a low power adhesive when trying to make a strong glue and for five years tried to promote it within 3M, but without success. One person whom he tried to interest was colleague Art Fry who sang in a choir and needed a way to mark places in his hymn book. Paper tabs with the not-very-sticky glue provided the answer. He used his 15%-time to turn the idea into a saleable product and by 1987 3M were calling it "one of the company's two or three most valuable assets".

Although the 15%-time rule apparently turned out to be anarchic and caused problems that later 3M management had to correct with the more structured Six Sigma process, the approach is now not uncommon in business. Enlightened managements recognise that organisational structures are often too inflexible to support world changing ideas that have no precedent.

Other firms' uses of bootlegging

Management guru Professor Peter Augsdorfer has studied the phenomenon encountered by 3M across many companies. He defines it as "unauthorised innovative activity that the employees themselves define and secretly organise" and he calls it *bootlegging*. One of his examples is of a scientist at GlaxoSmithKline who had an idea to improve a membrane filtration system. Despite discouragement from his manager, he developed the idea in paid company hours using company facilities over a long period of time. When the results of his work came out into the light, the value of his revolutionary product was recognised and it led to an investment of tens of millions of pounds.

Like GlaxoSmithKline, many companies do not recognise such practices formally, which is why they are often conducted in secret. To disguise the practice it often goes under a number of coded names such as *under the counter work, work behind the fume cupboard, Friday afternoon work, pet project* and many others. Whatever it is called, the objective is the same – for one or a small number of staff to prototype something that neither the management, nor the outside world, realise that they need yet.

One company that has topped 3M's 15%-time idea is Google, which has a 20%-rule. Marissa Mayer, Google vice president, says that the "20% time sends a strong message of trust to the engineers". She said that about half of new Google products originated in 20%-time. The practice started unofficially when Paul Buchheit conducted some experiments alongside his formal job. From them came prototypes for Gmail (the email program) and AdSense (the program that links advertisements with relevant searches). The latter innovation was crucial to the success of the company, since it provides its basic revenue model. From the 20%-time rule that Buchheit's successes inspired have come the other new products Google Suggest (auto-filled queries) and Orkut (a social network).

Critically, only companies with profitable core products like Google and 3M can support bootlegging, while smaller companies have to discourage the practice in order to keep unambiguous focus on the many essential tasks that must be done in order to survive. It is clear that 15% to 20% is significant surcharge on a company's salary bill for a service that may not yield viable results and even some established players deem it too high a price to pay. Apple used

> **"** Critically, only companies with profitable core products can support bootlegging. **"**

to have such a program, but has discontinued it, and does not offer side-project time to employees. 3M has recently been softening its stance by saying that the company has a 15% culture, rather than expecting all engineers to spend 15% of their time on bootleg projects. Even within Google there is tension between time that is spent on side projects to the detriment of the day job.

Nevertheless, it is certain that bootlegging will endure, whether it is practised in the open or hidden away in some corner. Even covert ventures are tolerated because good management recognises that an employee's natural curiosity can lead to better new product ideas than those that emerge from structured group analysis.

Effectuation

As noted earlier, Ed Roberts produced the Altair 8800 without having any idea who would buy it, or what they would use it for. In the event it pushed IBM into producing the PC which in turn created 10,000 millionaires amongst Microsoft employees by the year 2000. One of these was Rob Glaser, who took his money in 1994 with the intention of becoming involved with charitable works and civic projects. He wanted to promote his progressive politics and decided that the internet, plus Mosaic, plus 14.4kbps modems made streaming audio a possible route. As no one had done such a thing before there was no pattern to follow. He had said that he was not interested in the purely economic end of this "anymore than Pavarotti is interested in getting paid to sing", but he became rich just the same. He did not ever promote his political ideas through internet audio streaming but instead found another avenue to do this, by donating over $2.2 million to pro-Democratic organisations in the 2004 US election.

For Glaser, there was no way to make a business plan with a predetermined goal, because at that time there was no real-time audio streaming on the internet. There was no way to gauge market acceptance in a non-existent market. There could be no measurable risk, no statistical uncertainty, just an unknowable future. On the face of it, it was the worst possible situation, but only from the standpoint where plans are constructed to maximise expected returns after comprehensive analysis. Glaser did not have to construct such a plan, since he was going to invest his money into streaming audio anyway and see what goals emerged. This changed the picture completely.

Entrepreneurship and effectual reasoning

While Knightian uncertainty, with its unknowable future, does not allow us to predict a particular outcome as bystanders, if we *control* events then we do not need to predict the future – we can create it. This neat inversion is called *effectual reasoning* (causing things to happen) rather than *causal reasoning* (measuring the causes of external events). In the causal world, to the extent that we can predict the future, we can control it. With effectuation, to the extent that we can control the future, we do not need to predict it. In a position of Knightian uncertainty, people who base their decisions on effectuation have a market advantage because, unlike those who employ causal reasoning, they know where they are going.

Saras Sarasvathy, Associate Professor at the Darden Graduate School of Business Administration, University of Virginia, believes that effectuation is a powerful tool in expert entrepreneurial hands. She uses a simple cooking analogy to show the difference between the two styles of decision making:

> You can start from a recipe and follow it (*causal*), or you can look in the fridge and rustle up something with what you find (*effectual*).

Only by using the latter technique will anything new ever be produced. In the absence of similar products in established markets, it is the only way that such goods can be created. So, rather than predicting the future and following it, the entrepreneur needs the logic of control to create the market and thereby define the future. This makes prediction unnecessary, Knightian uncertainty is destroyed and surprises can be turned into advantages. This control of the future is achieved in three ways:

1. by influencing industry standards, which is made easier by being first,

2. by alliances and stakeholder commitments so that everyone is singing from *your* song sheet, and

3. by continual innovation, because a new industry is very unlikely to be right first time.

Sarasvathy believes that Rob Glaser was able to employ effectuation because his payoff from Microsoft enabled him to consider the affordable loss, rather than an expected return, for his venture. His ten years in the software business provided many opportunities to establish strategic partnerships despite the untried nature of the venture, and he could react quickly to unexpected events and benefit from them.

Sarasvathy and Suresh Kotha analysed Glaser's company RealNetworks, and its internet audio and video streaming products RealAudio, RealVideo and RealPlayer, against the effectuation criteria in *Dealing with Knightian uncertainty in the new economy: The Real Networks case.* They found that because Glaser was prepared to incur an affordable loss products were brought quickly to market, enabling RealPlayer to gain an 80% market share which as a result made RealNetworks products the de facto standards. Their products sat between the content providers and the computer software suppliers and so it was vital to have alliances to maximise the linkages between the two sides. This Glaser did to great effect with 150 strategic partnerships agreed in 29 months. Innovation was not neglected, with one-third of the staff engaged in research and development. By 1997, three years after its creation, the company had revenues of $36m and went public.

This example shows the power of effectuation for the entrepreneur, especially in the presence of an external driver as powerful as the internet. But as a company moves from start-up to established multinational, the market becomes mature and causal processes come to the fore. In early 2010, Rob Glaser the entrepreneur par excellence stepped aside from day-to-day management. McKinsey and Co. conducted a strategic review, and the company's management talked in the causal, and some might say contradictory, terminology of an "exciting roadmap for the future".

Game theory

Until now all of the proposed tools for handling change assume that a person or organisation is acting in isolation and that their actions have no effect on others. Game theory recognises that this is seldom the case and that the behaviour of the participants (players) can affect each other. The importance of interactions has been recognised informally for a long time. In 1787 James Madison, the fourth president of the USA, argued the case for acts of Congress rather than a system of independent state legislatures because "a unanimous and punctual obedience of 13 independent bodies, to the acts of the federal Government, ought not be calculated on" stating, among other things, that "a distrust of the voluntary compliance of each other may prevent the compliance of any, although it should be the latent disposition of all."

This is classic game theory thinking although it would not be recognised as such until 1944 with the publication of *Theory of Games and Economic Behavior* by John von Neumann and Oskar Morgenstern. Game theory likens decision making to making moves in a game and the outcome to the result of the game. Crucially the outcome for each participant or player depends upon the actions of all players. The tool has been applied to economics, political science, evolutionary biology and across a wide range of the social sciences, but for some there is a suspicion that it can be an academic's toy. Referring to Nash equilibrium, which is a key concept of game theory, it has been said:

> The math behind it is flawless and has transformed the way people think about evolution, arms races, stock market and tick-tack-toe. There's only one problem: People aren't rational.
>
> *Strategic Investment, Real Options and Games*, **Smit and Trigeorgis**

The auction as a game

One important game in business is an auction, where naturally the seller wants to sell for the maximum price and the buyer wants to buy for the cheapest price. For the seller, the two issues that matter with auction design are attracting entry and preventing collusion. A large number of potential buyers increases the competition, whereas collusion reduces competition. Unlike other branches of the science, game theory *does* have a solid and practical track record in the design of auctions, which has been revolutionised by its use.

The event which has recently taken such theories from academia to commerce is the auctioning in 2000-1 of the European 3G mobile telecommunications frequency spectra. Academics Ken Binmore and Paul Klemperer led the auction theorists advising the government agency which ran the UK segment of the auction. They later reviewed the whole process in *The Biggest Auction Ever: the Sale of the British 3G Telecom Licences*, on which the following is based:

> The sale was a one-off venture; the nine governments had little idea of the value of what they were selling and so they used auctions to get industry to reveal the value. The experiences illustrate both the rewards and pitfalls of the process. In total the auctions raised $100 billion, that is to say that this sum of money moved from the pockets of the shareholders to those of the European governments, but there was a greater than thirty-fold difference in revenues per head from the nine auctions. In the UK alone, £22.5 billion was raised, which amounted to 2.5% of GDP.

The UK was the first country to conduct its auction in March-April 2000 and the sale yielded €650 per head of population, which turned out to be the best achieved. Next came the Netherlands, which only yielded €170. The experience in Italy was similar, yielding only €240. Switzerland yielded the lowest return of all at €10 per head of population. In the German auction, Deutsche Telecomm, majority owned by the German government, pushed the revenues to 94% of the UK revenues at €615 per head, while Austria raised less than one-sixth of this. Before the final three auctions the technology bubble burst and with it the expectations for 3G networks. Belgium and Greece had to accept the reserve price of €45, while Denmark obtained €95 per head.

Analysing these wildly varying results, it is clear that the countries that designed the best forms of auction made the most money, although all were affected by the technology bubble and its bursting that coincided with the auctions. With so much money at stake bidders are going to try everything they can to turn things to their advantage, both by doing covert deals with their competitors and scaring them off as the opportunity occurs. The main contribution of game theory is to enable the sellers to put themselves in the shoes of the bidders and to think through all possible outcomes. For the European 3G Mobile licences the winning governments turned out to be those who were first to employ a particular design of auction (the UK, Germany and Denmark). Perhaps they caught the bidders before they learned the ropes.

In Summary

When disruptive changes happen, whether they are expected to happen or are deliberately triggered, planning is needed. However, conventional plans, which assume a single outcome and are formulated using historical information, are seldom suitable and more sophisticated alternatives must be sought. A natural tool which humans have always used in such circumstances is storytelling. This can be used to forewarn others of potential opportunities and dangers. It can also be used to construct stories in our heads of what might occur and these can be stored as memories of the future for subsequent recall.

A number of further tools have been devised, each of which have a part to play, depending on circumstances. Any disruption with no certain solution must be evaluated in order to select the correct tool for the job. If there is a probable solution that has not been completely identified, then the Delphi method or affinity diagrams are appropriate. If there are many possible solutions then either scenario planning or morphological analysis should be used. For those who are in a position to be able to engineer a particular solution, then the appropriate tool is effectuation for entrepreneurs; skunkworks or bootlegging for established players; and auctions for authorities. If the disruption is caused by a quality control problem then control charts can provide assistance.

Once the disruptive change has been completely tied down and its nature completely understood, then it can be turned into a product or a service in order to provide a useful function. This is a dangerous step as it requires a change in the mode of thinking, moving from the right-brain gestalt to left-brain serial logic. Tackling this challenge is the subject of Chapter 6.

Incubation – From Invention To Innovation

6

I do not think there is any thrill that can go through the human heart like that felt by the inventor as he sees some creation of the brain unfolding to success... Such emotions make a man forget food, sleep, friends, love, everything.

Nikola Tesla (1856-1943)

It is natural to think in terms of change occurring when a stable environment is suddenly and unexpectedly disrupted, but one of the most important transformations in business or in any organisation is when a disruptive change eventually settles down into a new more incremental pattern or even perfect stability. This is most often experienced in the development or exploitation phase of a new product or service that has been invented and which then needs to be industrialised.

In this book, this phase is referred to as innovation and is defined as the act of *introducing something new*. It has been called *new stuff that is made useful* and is distinguished from the more abstract process of invention, which is *creation of something new by ingenuity and imagination*. In the commercial world invention is the conversion of cash into ideas (R&D) and innovation is the conversion of ideas into cash (payback). Of the Benz couple we looked at earlier, Karl was the inventor and Bertha the innovator, while in the War of the Currents, Tesla was the inventor and Edison the innovator.

Others use the terms in slightly different ways. For Clayton Christensen, *disruptive innovation* describes a process by which a new product or service takes root, while *sustaining innovations* describes how existing products or services are enhanced. Michael Kirton's innovation is "the creation, acceptance and subsequent implementation of new ideas, concepts, processes, products, or services". In other words it covers both invention and innovation.

Companies and individuals that make the leap from invention to innovation have much in common, even though their businesses may be quite different. Often, as with Rob Glaser and RealNetworks, they move into markets that were simply not there before their arrival. New ideas often result in business models that disrupt other players; such as Amazon, which is crippling the traditional bookseller's business model. To achieve such a breakthrough, any new entrant's success must give customers better or more cost-effective options than they had before.

Transforming the bright idea or invention into the everyday product or service that can be delivered on time, efficiently and with a profit can be a difficult task, and invariably involves different skills and tools from those that created the initial spark. Challenges when making this transformation include funding crises and changing market conditions that threaten the viability of the project before the first unit can be sold. Initially Amazon was a loss-making venture and deep pockets were needed before it could overcome the status quo. In their way, these problems of implementation can be far more challenging than the well-defined puzzle of how to make the darned thing work.

This chapter will explain why the problems of implementation pose such difficulty and what is done to circumvent the problems.

We Could Be Zeros

A new invention or a new idea starts the disruptive change that it is hoped will result in producing something that is of value. In the *two speed world*, it is the change of gear and the failure to shift smoothly from generating new ideas (inventing) to productisation (innovation) that is the most common problem in getting successfully from idea to product. However, there are many other pitfalls that can slow progress or stop things completely. For instance, the

> **❝** In the *two speed world*, it is the change of gear and the failure to shift smoothly from generating new ideas (inventing) to productisation (innovation) that is the most common problem in getting successfully from idea to product. **❞**

idea might be trumped by a superior product. Outside interference, such as the government, might stop the progress, or insist on unreasonable conditions. Top management might fail to understand the potential for the new idea and starve it of sufficient resources. The development team might fail to translate the idea into a practical solution. The public might not want it. From this partial list it is easy to see that disruptive change always brings with it difficulties and this section provides some examples where the problems proved too much to handle.

A brief hover: cycles of business growth and contraction

In the 1950s Christopher Cockerell's hovercraft was a breakthrough idea, rapidly skimming over the water rather than ploughing through it. However, getting the concept from the drawing board to a commercial product was a big challenge for such a novel craft and there was a ten-year development period before car carrying hovercraft services across the English Channel started in 1968. Once established, regular product and service improvements were added until hovercrafts carrying more than 400 passengers and 60 cars were crossing the Channel in only 30 minutes.

The hovercraft had made it from the boffin's bright idea to a practical workaday service. However, the cross-Channel service ceased in 2000 after 32 years because in practice the invention proved to be inferior to the alternatives offered by traditional ferries, other innovative designs such as the catamaran and hydrofoil, and eventually the Channel Tunnel. In particular the Chunnel was the disruptor that did for the hovercraft. By 2010, except for the Solent crossing between Ryde and Southsea, passenger carrying hovercraft had disappeared from the coastline of Britain. So in a life cycle of approximately 50 years the device had gone from breakthrough idea to conventional commercial service to unwanted and outdated dinosaur.

This cycle is a recurrent pattern in the story of products and services, although the duration and the amplitude of any given cycle can be difficult to estimate. Many things that we assume will continue often disappear; these may be fashions, goods that become obsolete, services overtaken by more efficient new entrants (as we saw, train travel quickly supplanted canals) political movements and social mores. Often the demise of the product is followed by the failure of the company.

Readers who wish to pursue this subject further should read the book *Why Most Things Fail* by Paul Ormerod for many examples of this phenomenon. In it he quotes the British economic historian Leslie Hannah who, in a study of the world's largest companies of 1912, notes that by the end of the twentieth century the vast majority had disappeared. Past global giants such as Hohenlohe Iron & Steel, Briansk Rail & Engineering, Central Leather and Cudhay Packing are gone and totally forgotten. Indeed of the 100 top companies in 1912, 29 had gone bankrupt by 1995, and 48 had disappeared through mergers and takeovers. Of the 52 survivors, only 19 remained in the top 100.

Mixed and unclear objectives

One factor that often derails the incubation and development stage is mixed and unclear objectives. All too often governments are at the head of the line of miscreants in this respect. As shown earlier, government institutions have a tendency to plan and execute projects badly. The following cautionary tale of defence procurement in post-war Britain illustrates the issue well.

In the early 1960s, the UK military authorities were concerned that developments in surface-to-air missiles were rendering their existing fighters obsolete, so that the RAF needed a new strike aircraft solution to counter the threat. The technical puzzles were severe, but it was external management problems which sank the project, a point made succinctly by Sir Sydney Camm. He said: "All modern aircraft have four dimensions: span, length, height and politics. TSR-2 simply got the first three right."

Firstly, the government insisted that every bid be from more than one company. Their motive for this constraint was to encourage mergers among the UK's fragmented aerospace companies, but the consequence was to create design teams that were unfamiliar with each other's ways of working. Another initiative was to seek possible savings from combining the requirements of the Royal Navy and the RAF, but these came to nothing because of hostilities between the services. To cap it all, the Air Ministry insisted on designing some aspects itself, further confusing the process. The inevitable result was spiralling costs as changing specifications and mixed objectives invariably cause costs to expand. In April 1965 the TSR-2 programme was terminated, the aircraft having flown at supersonic speed just once. The rival American F-111K, which the government then selected to replace the TSR-2, itself suffered enormous cost escalation and severe teething troubles, so that in the end the RAF received neither plane.

The customer is not always right thinking

Customers do not always behave rationally and buy what is best for them, particularly when the object of their desires is the motorcar. People enjoy the freedom and excitement that car ownership brings, but sitting inside a two ton steel cage that is travelling at 70 miles an hour is inherently risky and logically drivers should welcome anything that reduces this risk. With this in mind, in 1956 the Ford Motor Company launched Lifeguard, a car safety package that included a safety deep-centre steering wheel, safety double-grip door latches, front and rear lap-only seat belts, padded dashboard and sun visors, recessed instruments and a safety rear-view mirror. The buying public was unmoved by the Lifeguard package and Henry Ford II remarked: "McNamara [Ford company president] is selling safety, but Chevrolet is selling cars."

Too late

Sometimes an invention, perhaps because of a changing environment, does not fulfil new requirements. Rabbit was a British location-specific telephone service, which was offered as an alternative to public call boxes, both of which only supported outgoing calls. Unfortunately by the time it was launched in 1992 mobile phones arrived with their ability to receive calls as well. This changed people's expectations and Rabbit did not enjoy a long life. At the height of its operations it only had 10,000 customers in the UK while it needed 12,000 base stations to support them. Unsurprisingly the service ceased only 20 months after being launched.

The mouse that got away

Palo Alto Research Center (PARC) is the flagship research division of the Xerox Corporation, founded back in 1970 by Jack Goldman, their chief scientist. Its first director was George Pake, a physicist specialising in nuclear magnetic resonance.

Palo Alto was 3000 miles away from Xerox headquarters and so in a way it was a skunkworks. The great distance meant that researchers could get on without interruption, but it also meant that their work went unnoticed by Xerox management who failed to see the potential of their innovations. In particular, critics point to the failure of Xerox to understand the significance of the work PARC was doing on the graphical user interface (GUI) and the desktop mouse. This functionality is now familiar to everyone, but it is associated in people's minds with Apple, IBM and Microsoft. Only computer buffs associate it with the name of Xerox.

Why then did Xerox fail to recognise the potential of the GUI and the mouse? Rowan Bunning, on reviewing Michael Hiltzik's *Dealers of Lightning and Complexity*, commented:

> To me, Xerox had all but blown it even before PARC was established! It would have taken nothing less than a wholesale reengineering of the whole corporation led by the board and top executives to give Xerox a chance. This sort of turnaround requires things like dramatic culture change.

Senior management needed to imagine all the possible futures that could befall the company, perhaps aided by a tool such as scenario planning (see Chapter 5). If they had then they might have recognised the opportunity when it came along. They might have recognised that going forward, to be successful on a large scale they would have to think small. That they had not thought this way is illustrated by a quote from the then head of PARC, Bob Taylor, who said, "A Xerox senior manager once said to me, if this is such a good idea, why isn't IBM working on it?" Of course they were in their own skunkworks in Boca Raton. So no one in Xerox moved until IBM released its unsophisticated but inexpensive PCs and by then the opportunity for Xerox was gone.

This illustrates the difficulty of getting an idea from the laboratory into the hands of the consumer, but for Xerox the full story is more complex. In the late 1960s Xerox was a huge company with a stranglehold on the copier industry. In their product development laboratory in Webster, New York, Gary Starkweather had an idea for an incremental enhancement to that business utilising a laser to paint an image onto the xerographic drum that was at its heart. Management thought that the idea was impractical and ordered him to desist, but he managed to get himself transferred to the newly created PARC, where he was able to continue his research.

At PARC Starkweather combined his original idea with character generation electronics and page formatting software to extend the copier into a complete printing solution. Although this represented a disruptive change to the computer business, it was no more than a logical enhancement of the copier business which Xerox management understood well. This understanding enabled Xerox to create a multibillion-dollar industry, thereby generating enough revenue to pay for PARC forever.

How the mighty are fallen

One important constraint for inventors and other entrepreneurs is something over which they have little control – the country in which they live. In Chapter 3 it was explained that the ideal environment for entrepreneurial activity was one with a well fed but under-employed population, sound intellectual property law and the absence of a totalitarian ruler. Such an environment is not permanently fixed and countries and regions go through periods of ascendancy, followed by prominence and then decline. A good example of this phenomenon is provided by the UK where there are signs that following the Second World War it is now well past the fruitful era that was triggered by the Agricultural and Industrial Revolutions. Are there lessons to be learned and can anything be done to reverse the trend?

The confidence of the UK in the nineteenth century can be gauged from the speed with which it developed its railway network. First the ports were linked to the places of manufacture and then quickly every community in the land was included. The statistics are amazing.

Robert Stephenson reported that by 1854, the aggregate length of the railways in Great Britain and Ireland was more than 8000 miles and that the earth that was moved to achieve this feat was equivalent to a cone of half a mile diameter and one and a half miles high. The capital raised for this frenzy of construction was £286 million. Around 20,000 men built the world's first inter-city railway line between London and Birmingham in five years. This makes a stark contrast with progress in the second half of the twentieth century.

After decades of neglect it took £9 billion and ten years to upgrade the London to Birmingham line. The new paymasters were the government, rather than Victorian capitalists, and they had to share the money with the new transport infrastructure, the road network. They also had to upgrade an existing and heavily used line rather than building across virgin ground. The justification for investment was always the cost of construction and operation against the revenue generated, while the bigger picture – which places a modern railway within a comprehensive transport system built to serve the whole population – was missing. The treatment of the railways in the UK is the symptom of a wider malaise, which is that the urgency and enthusiasm which characterised the Industrial Revolution seem to have gone somehow. It is as if the country has become middle-aged.

The UK is not the only country with signs of middle age lethargy. John Kao, American strategic advisor and author on innovation, is concerned about America losing its global lead. For him the warning signs are America's under-investment in physical infrastructure, its slow start on broadband, its poor public schools and the lack of welcome for immigrants. Curtis Carlson, Stanford

Research Institute head, is even more downbeat. He has said: "India and China are a tsunami about to overwhelm us." The only way out, Carlson insists, is "to learn the tools of innovation".

Such comments should be kept in perspective, since the USA is still the world's leading innovator and would-be usurpers often lack the legal infrastructure to encourage inventors, but Carlson's thoughts are indicative of worries that are surfacing. Every mature state sometimes needs a disruption to its steady progress to provide an incentive to cast off the staid bureaucracies with their *business as usual* mindset and to encourage more dangerous, youthful innovators.

Avoiding The Pitfalls

Up to this point in this chapter we have described some of the many ways in which the productisation of a disruptive idea can founder, and stressed the change of situation from getting the original spark of an idea to bringing it into life as a practical product. This mirrors the brain metaphor that was introduced in Chapter 1, where the initial idea needs the creativity of the right-brainers, while productisation needs the attention to detail of the left-brainers. For the innovation stage, the *productisation team* is selected with this in mind and is set to work within a framework which is generally controlled using a standard project management tool (thus suiting left-brainers). Money is secured, internally if the project is part of a larger organisation, externally if it is a start-up firm. Finally the potential product or service is ring fenced legally, so that the innovators rather than some imitator, benefits from the effort.

Picking the productisation team

The skills needed to tackle an innovation project containing novel problems and untried solutions are different in several respects from the skills needed to follow step-by-step procedures to complete a routine project. This is understood when recruiting an innovation team and special skills are sought out.

Almost all of the members are team players, who expect problems along the way but whose first reaction is to help solve the problem rather than accuse or punish the person that caused it. They are able to interact with people from a different background, who perhaps use unintelligible jargon and have different goals. Accountants must work with scientists; project managers must work with technicians.

Michael Kirton's approach to calibrating team members was introduced in Chapter 3. He has developed an instrument known as the KAI (Kirton Adaption-Innovation) Inventory, which measures the preferred problem-solving style of an individual as a single figure and uses this to calibrate team members. Both adaptor and innovator styles are needed in a team and the KAI inventory helps to get the balance right. As we saw, adaptors are efficient, thorough, adaptable, methodical, organised, precise, reliable, dependable, and respect rules and structure, whereas innovators are ingenious, original, independent, unconventional, less tolerant of structure (guidelines, rules) and less respectful of consensus.

Kirton found that a person at the adaptor end of the scale has difficulties understanding someone at the innovator end. A person who has an all-round ability to solve problems either as an adaptor or as an innovator is included on the team to act as a *bridger* between those at opposite ends of the scale. This person may also be the team captain, who is a strong leader (as with sports teams), and who acts as a broker between the other team members, knocking heads together when necessary.

The team captain also acts as the broker between the team and the outside world, interpreting the objectives of the board or sponsor, and understanding all of the implications for the project. Sometimes this means that the team captain has the unpleasant role of stopping the team from heading in the wrong direction. The team captain also acts as a shield, protecting other team members from outsiders who do not understand the special nature of the project and who complain when standard procedures are not being followed. Some organisations protect the team captain from this problem by hiding the team away from the mainstream business, as IBM did with the PC team and Lockheed did with the P-80 aircraft.

Since innovation is the object of the project, the team generally requires a *creative innovator*, typically an innovator in the KAI Inventory. This person may not be a team player, since by nature such people are dogmatic and are poor communicators. The rest of the team must accommodate this person's anti-social behaviour if the project is to reap the rewards of the innovator's ideas.

Another common team member is the *subversive*, who despite the name at least understands the ways of an adaptor in the KAI Inventory. This is the only member of the team who needs to have knowledge and experience of the mainstream parts of the organisation. Their role is to be a Mr or Ms Fixit, who works behind the scenes to get things done. They know the rules of the mainstream business and how to bend them to the needs of the project.

The other members of the team bring industry specific skills, such that the functional diversity covers all areas of the organisation affected by the project; commercial, technical and operations. This ensures that at every step questions can be asked from the viewpoint of the customer, the manufacturer and the salesman.

Over to the dead reckoners

Although innovation entails building something or offering a service that is quite new, it is certain that many of its components will be borrowed from existing product lines. For example, a new method for powering a motor car might be invented, but it is likely to be productised using bodywork, suspension, and indeed the majority of its components, from

> **"** All novelty is risky and so the greatest efficiency and the highest likelihood of success are obtained by limiting novelty to the area that is crucial to the invention itself. **"**

tried and tested conventional cars. As shown earlier, all novelty is risky and so the greatest efficiency and the highest likelihood of success are obtained by limiting novelty to the area that is crucial to the invention itself. When that is done, much of the project time is spent on conventional matters, which can be controlled using standard techniques. Having said that, the new idea will throw up unforeseen problems, at which point the plan must be set aside or reworked. Let's now look at the standard project management techniques.

Every project leader starts with the following routine questions at the outset:

- What is the objective?

- When is the start date?

- What resources are needed in addition to staff?

- Can it be done by the project team alone or are collaborators required?

- When will it be completed?

- What will it cost?

These are simple questions, but many projects have foundered where one or more were missed or glossed over. The Channel Tunnel is one of many prominent projects that have experienced a bumpy ride from idea to actuality and a long hard look before starting would have been valuable. In the event the total costs were nearly twice the forecast, owing to delays and changes. Lack of trust between the three main players (Eurotunnel, the constructors and the banks) made matters worse. The Safety Authority (whose budget it was not) insisted on meticulous safety precautions, causing further overruns. It might have been hoped that once the tunnel opened and the revenues started coming in its problems would be in the past, but unfortunately passenger demand was less than half the forecast level. This was partly because there was no high-speed rail link to London and because freight traffic was down on forecast by more than a third. In addition, competing airlines and ferries reduced their fares far below Eurotunnel's forecasts.

Financially painful experiences like the Channel Tunnel have encouraged the UK government and their contractors to employ structured methods in order to avoid recurrences of these problems with future projects. Project management is the definition of what needs to be done and calculating the best way to do it. As with the futurist tools discussed in Chapter 5, project management is no more than an aid in achieving this end though. It does ensure a logical, organised approach at every stage so that all the right questions are asked and the answers are not fudged, but it is not a magic bullet. A system called PRINCE2 (Projects in a Controlled Environment) has become the de facto project management standard used both by the UK Government and the international private sector.

Give me the money

Often it is a start-up company that attempts to convert the bright idea into a saleable product and for such ventures there is the additional problem of raising money to support the project before it becomes viable. There are a number of ways to achieve this and Dr Elizabeth Garnsey of Cambridge University has used the high-tech cluster of companies in Silicon Fen, Cambridge, to study the alternatives.

One of the companies, Acorn Computers, founded by Chris Curry and Hermann Hauser, struggled to make the transition from start-up to global company. Financing was required to get to the point where they had a saleable product and they had to overcome early cash-flow problems. The pair raised the finance on the back of a contract for the BBC Micro, but had to be rescued by Olivetti when they overestimated demand for Christmas 1984. Eventually Acorn, which had planned to make its own personal computers, joined up with Apple and VSLI technology to create ARM, a global company that designed the chip that powers most of the world's smartphones.

The near failure of Acorn illustrates the financial problems that come with rapid expansion. Dr Garnsey studied Acorn, together with fellow Cambridgeshire companies Sinclair Research Limited and Autonomy Corporation. As reported in the Observer in October 2009, she concluded that there are four alternatives to finance a technology start-up company: it can get its customers to finance it (Sinclair); it can license its intellectual property (ARM); it can raise money from venture capital firms (Autonomy); or it can obtain an early exit by finding a bigger company willing to acquire it (Acorn which was acquired by Olivetti, although through necessity rather than design).

Protecting the idea

Once sufficient funds have been acquired to take an inventive idea through the innovation stage, the next requirement is legal protection so that no one steals the idea. History is littered with tales of inventors unjustly handled. Edwin Drake struck oil in 1859 using modified techniques of the water drilling industry. At first no one knew what to do with so much oil and when a use was found Drake received little reward because he had patented nothing and consequently died a pauper. After a colourful life as a professional swimmer, stunt man and entertainer, in 1985 aged 48 Trevor Baylis started a new career as an inventor. He invented a variety of products to aid handicapped people. His line of Orange Aids helped people with limited mobility to hold onto and manoeuvre objects such as books and utensils more easily, but unfortunately others benefited from his ingenuity. He said afterwards:

> There is only one person I blame for getting shafted, and that's myself. I went into the deal which I thought would secure the future of Orange Aids with culpable impetuosity. I had been used to doing business on a handshake and my word of honour, and I made the error of actually believing what the men in the pin-striped suits told me.

Baylis did not make the same mistake with his best known invention, the wind-up radio, the lesser known wind-up walking stick or his electric shoes (though this last invention has been abandoned in the current era of heightened security, as shoes with wires in them are not welcome). Furthermore, he was determined that other lone inventors would get better protection than he did when he started out. In September 2003 he formed a company to help other inventors learn more about their inventions, how to go about protecting them and seek routes-to-market for the commercially viable ideas. To him the simple truth is that no one is master of all the necessary skills. He said:

> None of us have all the skills we need to bring products to the marketplace. So you need an incubator. Our job is to make sure that when the money rolls in, the inventor is not rolled out… We will then identify a route to market, make sure the intellectual property is put to bed properly, help come up with a good company name, and so on and so forth.

In Summary

Disruptive changes can occur in all walks of life, whether government, personal or business. One class of disruptive change is that triggered by a new invention and the implications of the gear change involved in this have been studied in the chapter. Once the full implications of an invention have been evaluated and the costs of implementation deemed to be worth spending, then the implementation can begin using an appropriate methodology such as PRINCE2. Although at this stage the hard creative work has been done, there are many further pitfalls along the way and since this is the most expensive phase, it is where the most money can be lost.

As we saw, during the building phase of the Channel Tunnel ferries and short-haul flights became cheaper, invalidating the original budget estimates. The fighter aircraft TSR-2 was beset by external government interference and only made one supersonic flight before it was cancelled. Although logic says that car drivers should value the lives of themselves and their families extremely highly, safety features failed to sell cars in the 1960s.

The expensive production phase must have the backing of top management. Xerox had a business model which was built around paper processing, so when they had a new opportunity in the paperless office there was a cultural hurdle that they could not clear. In a stable profitable company, top management may have a cultural dislike of any change at all.

In the face of these obstacles there are steps that can be taken to maximise the chance of success. Firstly, a team that includes all the necessary skills must be selected, for the inventor alone is no longer sufficient and indeed could be a hindrance in attending the birth of his/her baby. A reliable source of money must be secured that is sufficient to absorb any unexpected cost rises that result from overruns, raw material price rises, competitive price cutting and the myriad of other things that can occur as a project runs its course (unforeseen developments never seem to result in unexpected cost *falls*). Where necessary the ideas must be protected by law. A new invention often means a new market and so money must be set aside to educate both staff and customers.

Finally the innovator has to picture what effect the new product will have and ensure that everyone is prepared to fit it into their existing world. In an imagined telephone conversation with Sir Walter Raleigh, Bob Newhart tries to envisage innovative products from the New World and how they might be received in Elizabethan England:

> Are you saying 'snuff', Walt?... What's snuff?... You take a pinch of tobacco... and you shove it up your nose. Ha! ha!... and it makes you sneeze? Ha! ha! ha!... Yeh, I imagine it would, Walt!

7

Future Imperfect

Chance favours only the prepared mind.

Louis Pasteur (1822-1895)

An optimist judging the progress of human race would point out that it is doing pretty well. Up to this point many fantastic and sustained advances have been made and based on past results global prosperity should increase going forward. A pessimist might reply that the world is getting smaller and so the issues and challenges that face humanity are increasingly global problems, while the governments with the authority to solve the problems are national.

In concluding *Two Speed World* and tying together what we have discussed so far, we will focus our attention on the questions of whether the human race can really be confident going forward and what chances there are of progress in the future.

The Story So Far

Sextus Julius Frontinus (35-103AD) believed that by the first century AD everything that could be invented had already been invented. In fact, contrary to this Roman's view, it seems that the number of inventions is governed by the number of inventors, rather than by the number of things that are left to be invented.

The potential pool of inventors is the number of people with time to spare after satisfying their primary needs of providing food and shelter, and this in turn is related to the wealth of the world. For a long time the wealth of the world grew very slowly, with the per capita gross global product (GGP) advancing by only 50% from Roman times up to the Industrial Revolution. Thereafter it increased rapidly, advancing by a further factor of nine between 1820 and the end of the twentieth century. There were pockets of wealth throughout history and it was from them that early discoveries such as silk and glass working arose, but it was only from the beginning of the Industrial Revolution that the ingenuity of mankind was released and manmade disruptions proliferated.

> **Most people live from day to day in a world of incremental change and do not expect to be much affected by disruptive changes.**

Most people live from day to day in a world of incremental change and do not expect to be much affected by disruptive changes. For people who lived through the bulk of the twentieth century this perception was quite untrue, as the changes that they witnessed just in the fields of communications and air/space travel show (see Table 7.1).

Table 7.1 – Twentieth century dvances in communications and air/space travel

Year	Communications	Air/space travel
1901	First wireless communication between UK and USA.	
1903		First flight by Wright brothers.
1909		First flight across English Channel; first military reconnaissance aircraft.
1914		First scheduled commercial flight.
1919		First flight across Atlantic.
1920	First public radio station.	
1927	First talkie film.	First solo flight across Atlantic.
1935	Radar invented.	
1929	First public television broadcast (UK).	
1939		Helicopter invented.
1945	First computer built.	
1953	First colour TV.	
1964	First commercial time-sharing computer system.	
1969	ARPANET created.	First men on the moon.
1971	Video recorders.	
1972	First email.	
1975	First personal computer MITS Altair 8800.	
1981	IBM PC.	
1991	World Wide Web.	
1995	Amazon started.	
1998	Mobile phones and internet commonplace.	

In Play

There is no sign that the pace of technological advance set in the twentieth century is slackening in the early years of the twenty-first century – there is every reason to expect this pace to be maintained, or even to accelerate for as long as the wealth of the world remains high. Additionally, nature will add disruptions from time to time as it always has.

Let us now look at some isolated examples of disruptions that are in play at present to illustrate the range of possible sources – nature, human ingenuity, government, nature/human interaction – of disruptions.

Natural violence

Nature is always capable of delivering devastating disruptions through volcanoes, earthquakes, tsunamis and extreme weather. In 1783 a volcanic eruption in Iceland killed one-fifth of the population and reputedly poisoned 23,000 Britons. In Chapter 3, the dangers posed by Mount Vesuvius were described and the fact that they are ignored by the two million people who live there and the hundreds of thousands of annual visitors. The authorities have an emergency plan, which assumes between 14 and 20 days notice of an eruption, but vulcanologists say that they cannot promise to provide that. The evacuation is planned to take about seven days and to remove 600,000 people from the area, but the dilemma that would face those implementing the plan would be when to start this massive evacuation.

If the evacuation is left too late then many people could be trapped, but if it is started too early then it could turn out to be a false alarm, which is what happened in 1984 when 40,000 people were evacuated from the surrounding area of another Neapolitan volcano, only for no eruption to actually occur. Balancing the competing demands of vulcanologists, politicians, transport authorities, local pressure groups and others would appear to be an ideal task for the morphological analysis tool that was described in Chapter 5, but in the meantime ongoing efforts are being made to reduce the population living in the danger zone so that the time needed to evacuate the area is reduced to two or three days. It is intended that some of the houses emptied in this way will be converted into bed and breakfast hotels, but the reason for the properties being vacant will probably not be included in the holiday brochures.

Where man and nature collide

In the past 2000 years, humankind has been extremely successful at propagating itself, with the world population growing from a quarter of a billion in Roman times, to one billion at the start of the Industrial Revolution and on to more than six billion in 2010. This, plus the changes that humans are themselves causing, is starting to test the capacity of the world to support us. In *The Meaning of the 21st Century*, James Martin – a computer scientist and futurologist – identified four crises that could upset the balance of the whole planet, namely: food shortage, climate catastrophe, water shortage and fuel shortage. Here we will examine just one of these threats – water shortage – and how such a crisis might unfold.

A potential water shortage crisis

Everyone needs to drink around two litres of water every day in order to stay alive, but this is a very small part of the total amount of water that is used every day in the world. To make this important point easy to visualise, Professor Tony Allan of King's College London uses the concept of virtual water to denote the amount of water used in the complete production process for different foodstuffs, making very clear the necessity of water for human survival. The amount of virtual water that is needed for common products includes 70 litres for an apple, 1000 litres for a litre of milk and 2400 litres for a hamburger.

The vital role of water has been understood from earliest times. Every community has grown up around a water source and its capacity has determined the size of the community that could be supported. It is quite clear that a water supply is something which Ancient Rome, with its population of one million people, understood well. As water commissioner for the city, Sextus Julius Frontinus produced an official report, 'The Aqueducts of Rome', in 97-8AD. It was the first official report about engineering works ever to have been published. His recognition of their importance was clear from the following boast: "With such an array of indispensable structures carrying so many waters, compare, if you will, the idle Pyramids or the useless, though famous, works of the Greeks!"

Generally the sources for this life-giving resource are the rivers that run through or near the communities served, but rivers typically pass through several countries and are often used as national boundaries and so there is potential for arguments over extraction of water these sources. The Nile, by some measures the longest river in the world, flows through nine countries, but a 1959 treaty means that only Egypt and the Sudan are entitled to its waters. In the 1960s, at the height of the Cold War, President Nasser of Egypt built the Aswan High dam with Russian technical assistance and money. This controls the flow of water through Egypt and generates much of its energy, but it holds back the silt that once fertilised the land. Furthermore its reservoir, Lake Nasser, in the glare of the desert sun, loses around a quarter of the river's entire flow through evaporation. Earlier engineers planned to avoid this problem through a series of dams upstream in the mountains of Ethiopia, but Nasser wanted an Egyptian dam on Egyptian soil.

If Nasser so desired a landmark project to make his name perhaps he should have stuck to building pyramids, but then Egypt is not alone in placing national prestige and local interests before common sense. Many solutions to water problems are best solved by small, local projects – modest reservoirs used to be built and maintained by local villagers and for a millennium they provided water in times of need – but today politicians like grandiose projects with which they can make their name.

The status of water as being second only to air in supporting life means many people believe it to be a human right that no one should have to pay for. This belief skews water economics so that it is not used optimally. As long ago as the sixth century the Byzantine emperor Justinian declared that by natural law air, running water, the sea and seashore were *common to all*. As a consequence, the embedded cost of water in doing such things as producing a crop is hidden and, as a free resource, water is used indiscriminately. This naturally builds up problems for the future. For example, in India the 20 million well-users are causing the water table to fall at an average of 3 to 10 feet per year.

Up to this point in human history water has posed an incremental problem, with demand rising steadily year by year, but because it is essential to life at the most fundamental level there is the ever-present danger that it will become a disruption. Water does not recognise national boundaries, meaning that this disruption could occur anywhere in the world where there are shortages and so the issue must be addressed internationally.

This needs to be recognised as a *mess*, as defined in Chapter 3, with widely differing contributing factors, including climate change, political friction and technical solutions that affect both water's supply and demand. In the face of such complexity, a wide margin of error must be included in any estimates that are made. The full water requirement must be estimated using the concept of virtual water so that the notion of every human's right to free water does not obscure the true costs of its provision. Such integrated thinking will prevent virtual water from being exported from countries that are short of water, by such means as using crops like sugar-beet in dry regions to make biofuels.

A huge amount of freshwater falls as rain every day, but most of it drains to the sea where it is lost. There are exciting technical opportunities to improve the situation, but unfortunately most of the areas of the world that are in most urgent need of water are unlikely to come up with the solutions. Africa, with its extensive desert areas, has a per capita GGP of only one-seventeenth that of the West. As a continent it can give too few people the time and the resources needed in order to devise the necessary technical solutions locally.

An Englishman's car is his chariot

Since Karl Benz produced the first practical petrol-driven motorcar in 1885 with its solid tyres, three wheels, single gear and tiller steering, thousands of enhancements have changed motoring out of all recognition. It has improved by every measure, becoming safer, cheaper, faster, more reliable and more comfortable. There are now 900 million cars and light trucks in the world (one for every seven people), and directly and indirectly the motorcar provides a livelihood for millions of people in car manufacture and maintenance; in oil exploration, refining and distribution; and in road building and infrastructure maintenance. And yet there could be trouble ahead.

Hostile critics falsely claimed in 1972 that the Club of Rome predicted that oil would run out in 1992. We know this did not happen and oil is unlikely to run out in such a dramatic fashion, but it is already becoming more difficult and more expensive to extract and this will result in steadily rising real prices. It is problematic that much of the world's oil is situated in politically unstable regions and so major oilfields could become unavailable for significant periods of time. Also, when burned, oil contributes to global warming and causes air pollution, which is unpleasant and dangerous to the inhabitants of towns. It is possible, then, that one day oil could be deemed an unacceptable energy source when considering the wellbeing of the world and the people in it.

The industry incumbents have responded to these difficulties with incremental improvements that, when added together, represent a tremendous advance in efficiency and cleaner running. As just one indication of how importantly the industry takes this, Progressive Insurance, an American insurance company, offered a prize of $10 million for the first passenger vehicle capable of operating at 100 miles per gallon, that is safe, affordable and which people want to buy. There were 136 cars entered into the competition.

Established market players will continue to make incremental improvements in order to avoid the major disruption that could displace them, but that may not be enough to satisfy public opinion and legislation could result in demands for something more dramatic. This would present the upstarts with their opportunity. Some technical alternatives already exist, with hybrid engines reducing pollution in towns and electric and fuel cell power offering the opportunity to move away from hydrocarbon fuels altogether. What we know about disruptive innovation (see Chapter 3) suggests that if an old order is to be overthrown – if there is to be dramatic change – it will be caused by upstarts getting a toehold at the bottom of the market. This might be in the introduction of a new run-about vehicle for local journeys, say, which initially has little impact on the overall market but then moves into the mainstream from there.

Dictatorship of the minority

Disruptions can be purely political. The UK, in company with the USA, Canada and France, uses a first past the post (FPTP) voting system for their general elections. This is not a universally popular system and has been dubbed a *dictatorship of the minority*. Most of the rest of Europe (and indeed the UK for its regional governments, European parliament representatives and election of the Mayor of London) uses some variant of the proportional representation (PR) voting system. In general, the established parties prefer FPTP since it enables them to form an unfettered government without securing an absolute majority, which is precisely why smaller parties who are trying to unseat the big boys prefer PR. The USA flirted with PR after the Second World War, but the two main parties fought back with Cold War scare stories suggesting that such a system was radical and un-American and would result in electing Communists, Socialists and the like.

In the UK, in 1998, the Jenkins Commission looked for an alternative to the existing system. It came up with Alternate Vote Plus (AV+). This system would provide individual MPs to represent 500 constituencies who would be elected using the AV system. To provide better proportionality, the constituency MPs would be topped up by MPs who would be elected from regional party lists and allocated in a way that balances the ratio of votes to constituency seats. The system is complicated and potentially confusing to voters, and furthermore it can be gamed by dividing a political party into two, with one half providing the bulk of the constituency list and the other half providing the county list.

Nevertheless, the proposal does provide a degree of PR and so when it was published the two main parties opposed the recommendation, while the smaller parties, the Liberal Democrats and the SNP, welcomed it. The promised referendum on the proposal did not happen at the time, but the idea has been resurrected and any change in the electoral system for general elections would represent a significant disruption that would trigger a number of changes in the working of national politics in the UK. For example, the likelihood of coalitions would be increased, so that there would be less chance of extreme policies, though in some proportional systems extreme parties have got small numbers into legislatures.

Political scenarios – including the potential for electoral reform – must be kept in mind at both the personal and the business level in order to be ready for such an eventuality.

Fast Forward

Most of life must be lived at the slow speed of incremental change, following Established Practice, to ensure both personal and group survival. Occasionally, though, things speed up in a way that may at the time be traumatic, but over the long run ensures progress rather than stagnation. The secret is to maintain the correct balance between the two speeds and not become locked onto one speed to the detriment of the other.

Every person and every business should regularly review their situation and not assume that the future will continue as a simple extension of the present state. In particular, they should differentiate between a disruptive change and a large, but nevertheless incremental, change, for a wrong diagnosis can result in a wrong remedy. The financial crisis of 2007-2009 was interpreted by some as an extreme but well understood situation, which blew up because the rules which normally kept the system within bounds were not applied rigorously enough, or were incomplete. Based upon this interpretation

> **“** Every person and every business should regularly review their situation and not assume that the future will continue as a simple extension of the present state. **”**

more rules were required to fill the holes. On the other hand, if the situation was wrongly assessed and the existing rules were inappropriate and actually fed the instability, then more rules are likely to exacerbate the situation next time. If the linkages connecting the sectors of the financial world are only partially understood then the situation is a mess (a complex issue which is not well defined) and it must not be treated as a puzzle (a well-defined problem with a specific solution).

Throughout this book we have utilised a series of simple contrasts to explain our argument – two speeds, disruptive or incremental change, and left-brain or right-brain thinking. In the context that they are used, these simplifications are valid and they enable some very powerful points to be made. However, we have also repeatedly warned of the dangers of stretching assumptions too far and care must be taken when employing this series of simple contrasts also.

The book creates a black and white world that is populated solely by mavericks and box tickers, but this is sometimes a dangerous over-simplification. In particular, the crucial *grey* people who have a foot in each camp and are sympathetic to both points of view cannot be omitted. These *greys* form the bridge between the two extremes, providing explanations, fostering understanding and countering the antagonism of one side to the other. They tackle C. P. Snow's problem of the two cultures and without them the *blacks* and the *whites* would cancel out each other's contribution. Everyone should be prepared to take this bridging role in their lives, for disruptions arise at all levels – in personal life, in the work place, in national government and in international co-operation.

For example, family friction might arise between a teenager and a grumpy old man. Discord at work might arise between those staff who need to make their numbers and those with a looser brief who can apparently get away with anything. A sudden influx of immigrants might be viewed differently by a government department who needs their skills and MPs in the constituencies where they must be housed. The use of generic AIDS medicine is a good thing for poor countries suffering an epidemic, but a bad thing for pharmaceutical companies hoping to recover their development costs.

Aware and ready

Every individual must be prepared for the challenges ahead. No one should say "It cannot happen to me!" or "Sufficient unto the day is the evil thereof" but rather everyone must be poised for any sudden change in their situation, whether for better or worse.

When people apply for jobs it is common for personality tests to be used as part of the evaluation process, perhaps based upon the KAI inventory, or the *big five* traits of openness, conscientiousness, extraversion, agreeableness and neuroticism, that were described in Chapter 3. This is used to indicate the applicant's suitability, with a high *openness* score indicating a strong creative side, and a high *conscientiousness* score indicating an ability to attend to detail and follow rules.

Individuals starting out in adult life use the same tests to help them choose their general career path. Education and training generally determine a person's subsequent career trajectory. For those with no firm career objectives, further education is undertaken in general disciplines in order to be ready for any opportunity that arises. Training for a specific career provides higher job security as long as the world and the person's place within it remain relatively constant. The security disappears for someone who trains as a jockey and then gains a lot of weight. A general education can make it difficult to get started, but the extra flexibility makes it easier to deal with changing circumstances as time goes by.

Those settled into a career continue to watch for potential disruptions. If there are redundancies in a firm, or if its products are being pushed aside by the competition, it must be decided whether these developments are within the normal run of events, or whether they signal a sea change and suggest that a career move would be sensible. For instance, if mines are closing and jobs in that industry are being cut, perhaps it is better to retrain or emigrate rather than attempt to become a better miner.

Finally, like Shell and the scenario planners, individuals need to take time out to read, tell themselves stories and ask "What if…?" Day dreaming is not a waste of time, but in fact it is the way that humans build memories of the future, imagining what may befall them and in that way preparing themselves for anything that might occur.

King or young pretender

People working in the private sector must always be sensitive to the threats and opportunities that possible disruptions might cause and how they might affect their company. If the company is mature, with well respected products in an established market, then there is every incentive to maintain the status quo. All of the facts, knowledge and skills that the company has gathered mean that it is more difficult for newcomers to challenge the established players. The lessons from the Chinese silk industry and Venetian glassware production show that any disruptive change can make a company's experience redundant overnight and leave it with a workforce that is inflexible and which the years of stability have made resistant to change.

In a situation where a maintenance of the status quo is desired, it is achieved by developing processes that are efficient because they are repetitive, with apprenticeships and other focussed training schemes; developing products that by incremental improvements appeal to the existing customer base; and improving quality with tools like the control chart (see Chapter 5). Outside the factory walls, the company will support legislation that prohibits encroachment onto its territory, and will be active in national associations that showcase and lobby for the existing product line. The horse-driven coach trade and the railways fought against the newcomer that was road traffic. The result was the Red Flag Act of 1865, which insisted that every road vehicle had a three-man crew, including the famous man with the red flag. Although ostensibly one of the reasons for the legislation was to avoid frightening the horses, there were reports that the waving flag frightened them anyway.

If the company is young and is trying to break into an existing market, or create a new market, then the opposite is true and disruptions are encouraged. The company will get the sympathy of the general public, who benefit in the long term from Schumpeter's creative disruptions. DEC illustrated both the example of a young company breaking into an existing market and then of a mature company that was undermined by the next disruption. DEC's breakthrough against the established might of IBM and the other mainframe companies came with its introduction of time-sharing computers, and its demise arrived 40 years later when the new 'new boys' arrived with networked personal computers.

DEC provides the salutary lesson that even established players need to be on the constant lookout for external disruptions, particularly if they operate in the high-technology arena. Such a company needs to include planners on its staff that do not simply take past production and market data and extrapolate them forward, but rather imagine the outcome arising from sudden disruptions for which there is no history. Tools such as scenario planning and morphological analysis can put structure into these exercises, enable the planning experts to harness the ideas from many sources and create a collective daydream.

Once a possible new direction has been glimpsed, it must be nurtured and this can be difficult in an organisation that has been honed to deliver the existing product line in the most efficient manner. Every company needs a number of mavericks who are ready to try something different. The company should encourage these mavericks to get involved with independent projects in the style pioneered by 3M, or set up separate centres as done by IBM, Xerox and Lockheed. When this is done the hardest stage is absorbing the project back into the mainstream of the company's operations, with its production and sales targets, and with the competition for resources from the standard product line.

Handling disruptions must be kept in perspective. In most companies, the majority of people are concerned with the day-to-day activities connected with the established products and although there is always a need for creative thinking, most people are engaged in routine tasks and thinking inside the box. Although putting all the creative thinkers together and keeping them away from the mainstream is a technique that can be used in some situations, this can create a *them and us* dichotomy. In some circumstances there are more benefits from not having high walls between departments – on the contrary it can be good to have a few creative people in departments that are mostly concerned with routine and vice versa. Such people can act as go-betweens and perform important roles including explaining ideas and assumptions to decision makers and implementers.

Every company is composed of employees, who all possess the human frailties of bias and irrationality, and these traits are particularly pronounced when personal goals do not coincide with company goals. This can result in people defending their own projects when they should be cancelled and recommending that positions in markets be preserved when they should be given up. Tools such as the Delphi method should be used to get a less biased picture and to indicate the rational course to follow.

National championship

The government has a vital role to perform in supporting a mixed community of routine followers and mavericks. It must provide a safety net to deal with disruptions that are too large for individuals and corporations to handle, such as terrorist attacks, wars, pandemics and systemic failures of parts of the economy. Government generally operates in an incremental way, collecting taxes, passing laws which trim the existing ones and looking after state-controlled institutions. Occasionally government triggers a disruption by passing legislation that changes behaviour completely – such as changing the traditional voting rules – and occasionally it reacts to disruptions such as hostile foreign activity.

In theory the government could tackle projects directly, but government timescales do not fit well with project requirements. Logically government should only tackle projects that are too large for private enterprise to tackle, but such projects last longer than a government's term of up to five years (in the case of the UK) and much longer than the tenure of the minister responsible. For that and other reasons the government track record in running projects is not good (see the findings of Professor D. R. Myddelton in Chapter 3) and so government projects should only be undertaken directly in exceptional circumstances.

What the government must provide is an environment that encourages enterprise. It should provide both first class general education and specific training which matches the needs of the nation. It should provide strong legal protection of intellectual property rights in order to encourage both individual and corporate inventors. Here the UK has a good record, with the first patent law being enacted in 1623. It should also encourage start-up companies with tax incentives and other favourable treatment, since it is from them that the next generation of inventions and innovation will come.

> **Government must provide both first class general education and specific training which matches the needs of the nation.**

What the government should not do is to tinker with economic practice for political reasons. US politicians had the admirable objective to help people on lower incomes achieve home ownership and passed legislation to force lenders to give them loans. The consequence was a financial crash that hurt not just them, but the entire Western world.

The role of government should not be underestimated and if it loses its entrepreneurial focus it can preside over a country which loses its innovative edge and becomes *middle aged*. John Kao (Chapter 6) detects that this is even happening in the USA, which has been the most innovative country during the last century.

Global village

Early man probably shared all resources and lacked the concept of ownership, while Justinian in the sixth century AD still believed that running water, the sea and seashore were common to all. However, by 1968 Garrett Hardin postulated that any resource that lacked a clear owner would be destroyed by the selfishness of individuals, who never act for the collective good. In 'The Tragedy of the Commons', Hardin uses the metaphor of the village commons where a man will add a further grazing cow, because he enjoys a benefit, even though he knows that if a common has too many cows, everyone else loses.

Although historians challenge whether Hardin's model really holds true, the application of the metaphor to sustainability is widely acknowledged and the dilemma stands as a model for a great variety of resource problems in society today, such as water, land, fish, and non-renewable energy sources like oil and coal. This echoes the thoughts of James Madison in 1787 when he said the 13 states at the time could not be trusted to act voluntarily for the common good of the USA. The conclusion to be drawn from this is that many of the problems that could burst into a disruptive change are global in nature and need to be tackled in a co-ordinated fashion.

For instance, the UK may conclude that nuclear energy is too risky to use, but when France concludes otherwise and sites a nuclear power station at Gravelines, just 45 miles from the English mainland, Britain is in danger anyway. In the absence of a world government, these dangers threaten huge disruption and yet must be tackled by disparate groups with widely differing priorities.

Communities that are least able to deal with problems are often those that experience the greatest threats from the problems, for example the potential water crisis. Perhaps when the World Bank provides a loan to such a country, rather than insisting that it adopt Western-style democracy as a precondition, it should insist that the country introduces an environment that is conducive to inventors, including good universities and rigorously policed intellectual property rights. This is important because, while the use of supranational centres of knowledge and invention will undoubtedly be useful for dealing with future problems that transcend national boundaries (such as the water issue we have covered, or an oil shortage) the areas most affected will need people at the sharp end – within the area itself – working to solve the problems too.

> **Even disruptions that eventually are a benefit to all produce some short-term pain.**

Slow, Slow, Quick, Quick, Slow

This chapter seems to consist of a lot of bleak warnings and predictions of impending disasters. Even disruptions that eventually are a benefit to all, like the provision of a worldwide information and data processing network, produce some short-term pain, such as the demise of DEC. That said, while the wealth of the world is increasing, new ideas will continue to emerge and the successful ones will drive overall progress. The challenge is to ensure that this positive trend stays ahead of the natural and manmade disasters that create negative shocks.

Overall it is an exciting time to be alive and indeed, in the opinion of James Martin, it is the most exciting time ever. After considering other exciting times in history such as London in the Shakespeare years, the Paris of La Belle Époque, the Athens of Pericles and the Florence of Michelangelo, he concluded:

> If I could choose any time to live, I would want to be a teenager now (in a country where great education is available). There is excitement in the air – perhaps more excitement than at any other time… The most important reason I would choose today is that, more than at any other time, young people will make a spectacular difference.

Final Thoughts

Humans might be considered to be at a disadvantage to other mammals on earth, for there is nothing that our species is particularly good at. Many species are physically adapted to run fast, climb high, swim, or fly. Other species have their brains preprogrammed with instincts for nest building, hunting and avoiding predators. Crucially, though, humans have the single advantage of flexibility and that has turned out to trump all of the other abilities and skills. Humans have developed pseudo-instincts through Established Practice to create hunter humans, farmer humans, fisher humans, but the thing which differentiates them from true specialists such as the buffalo, lion and heron is that if conditions change then, through a disruptive change, humans can reinvent themselves as something else completely.

Today most humans are not so close to nature, but the ability to specialise, and when necessary switch, remains a defining characteristic of the human race and its continued success depends upon never forgetting this fact.

References

Chapter 1: From Here to Uncertainty

Eldredge, N. and Gould, S. J., 'Punctuated equilibria: an alternative to phyletic gradualism' in *Models in Paleobiology*, T.J.M. Schopf (ed.), (Freeman Cooper, 1972), pp. 82-115.

Kahneman, Daniel and Tversky, Amos (eds.), *Choices, Values, and Frames* (Cambridge University Press, 2000). For behavioural economics.

Coates, John and Herbert, Joe, *Endogenous steroids and financial risk taking on a London trading floor* (Proceedings of the National Academy of Sciences USA, April 2008).

Knight, Frank H., *Risk, Uncertainty and Profit*, Hart, Schaffner and Marx Prize Essays, no. 31. (Houghton Mifflin, 1921).

Arnold-Baker, Charles, *The Companion to British History* (Routledge, 2001), pp. 1231. For canal mania and railway mania.

Sperry, Roger W., 'Some Effects of Disconnecting the Cerebral Hemispheres', Nobel Lecture, 8 December 1981.

McCrone, John, ' "Right Brain" or "Left Brain" – Myth or Reality?', *The New Scientist*, RBI Limited 2000.

Snow, C.P., 'The Two Cultures and the Scientific Revolution', Rede Lecture, 7 May 1959. Subsequently published as *The Two Cultures* (Cambridge University Press, 1960).

McGilchrist, Iain, *The Master and His Emissary* (Yale University Press, 2009).

Chapter 2: Dead Reckoning

'Bellarmine to Foscarini', *Opere* 12 (12 April 1615), pp. 171-2 (abridged), from *Discoveries and Opinions of Galileo*, trans. Stillman Drake (Doubleday, 1957), pp. 162-4.

Neri, Antonio, *The Art of Glass: wherein are shown the wayes to make and colour Glass, Pastes, Enamels, Lakes, and other Curiosities* (Octavian Pulleyn, London, 1662) trans. (with some observations on the author) Christopher Merrett.

Culpeper, Nicholas, *Complete Herbal: A Book of Natural Remedies of Ancient Ills* , (The Wordsworth Collection Reference Library, NTC/Contemporary Publishing Company, 1995).

Links, J.G., *Venice for Pleasure* (Pallas Athene, 1997).

Meadows, Donella H;, Meadows, Dennis L.; Randers, Jørgen; and Behrens III, William W., *The Limits to Growth* (Universe Books, 1972). The book was commisioned by the Club of Rome.

Simmons, Matthew R., *Revisiting the Limits of Growth: Could the Club of Rome have been correct, after all?* (Simmons and Company International, 2000).

Chapter 3: Disruptive Change

O'Reilly, Tim, 'Jeff Bezos at Wired Disruptive by Design Conference', Biz Deans Talk: A Discussion on Management Education, **www.deanstalk.net/deanstalk/2009/06/tips-on-innovation-enterprenuership-from-jeff-bezos.html** (2009).

Ackoff, Russell, *Redesigning the Future: A Systems Approach to Societal Problems* (John Wiley & Sons, 1974).

Pidd, Michael, *Tools for Thinking* (John Wiley & Sons, 1996).

Dobran, Flavio, 'Vesuvius: the making of a catastrophe', Global Volcanic and Environmental Systems Simulation (GVES) Brochure. (For online copy see **www.westnet.com/~dobran/Brochure.html**.)

Taleb, N.N., *The Black Swan* (Penguin, 2008). For a criticism of the book see the blog of Professor David Aldous, University of California, Berkeley (**www.stat.berkeley.edu/~aldous/157/Books/taleb.html**).

Schumpeter, J., *Capitalism, Socialism and Democracy* (Routledge, 1994), originally published in 1942.

Christensen, Clayton, *The Innovator's Dilemma* (Harvard Business School Press, 1997).

Deutschman, Alan, 'Building a Better Skunk Works', *Fast Company Magazine* 92 (1 March 2005).

Myddelton, D.R., 'They Meant Well, Government Project Disasters', The Institute of Economic Affairs monograph, 2007.

Vujovic, Ljubo, 'Nikola Tesla, The Genius who Lit the World', Tesla Memorial Society of New York, 1998 (**www.teslasociety.com/biography.htm**).

Galton, Francis, 'Psychometric Facts', *Nineteenth Century* (March 1879), pp. 425-33.

Kirton, M.J., *Adaption-Innovation in Context of Diversity and Change* (Routledge, 2002).

Ee, Jessie; Seng, Tan Oon; Kwang, Ng Aik; 'Styles of Creativity: Adaptors and Innovators in a Singapore context', *Asia Pacific Education Review* 8:3 (December 2007), pp. 364-373.

'AIDS, Drug Prices and Generic Drugs', AVERT (**www.avert.org**), 2010.

Lipscomb, Andrew A. and Bergh, Albert Ellery (eds.), *The Writings of Thomas Jefferson*. 20 vols. Washington: Thomas Jefferson Memorial Association, 1905. Letter to Isaac McPherson, vol. 13, 13 August 1813, pp. 333-35.

Fisk, Robert, 'Why does life in the Middle East remain rooted in the Middle Ages?', *Independent* (28 July 2009).

Mankiw, Greg, *Principles of Economics* (Southwestern College, 2006). On resale price maintenance.

Pollock, Ian, 'Not Such a good Idea after all?', BBC News, **news.bbc.co.uk/1/hi/business/7641925.stm** (29 September 2008).

Chapter 4: Cascades and Consequences

Leiner, Barry M.; Cerf, Vinton G.; Clark, David D.; Kahn, Robert E.; Kleinrock, Leonard; Lynch, Daniel C.; Postel, Jon; Roberts, Larry G.; Wolff, Stephen, 'A Brief History of the Internet', Internet Society (ISOC), **www.isoc.org/internet/history/brief.shtml**

Gorz, André, 'The Social Ideology of the Motorcar', *Le Sauvage* (September-October 1973).

Tranter, Paul J. and Doyle, John W., 'Reclaiming the Residential Street as Play Space', *International Play* 4 (1996), pp. 91-97.

Chapter 5: The Futurist's Toolbag

Ingvar, D. H., 'Memory of the future: an essay on the temporal organization of conscious awareness', *Human Neurobiology* 4 (1985), pp. 127-136.

de Geus, Arie, *The Living Company* (Longview Publishing Limited, 1997).

Schwartz, Peter, *The Art of the Long View* (Doubleday, 1991).

Garfield, Simon, *The Last Journey of William Huskisson* (Faber and Faber, 2002).

'A Futurist's Toolbox: Methodologies in Futures Work', Performance and Innovation Unit, Cabinet Office, September 2001.

'Biography of Kawakita', citation for the 1984 Ramon Magsaysay Award for International Understanding, September 1984, Manila (**www.rmaf.org.ph/Awardees/Biography/BiographyKawakitaJir.htm**).

Kahn, Herman and Weiner, Anthony, *The Year 2000: A Framework for Speculation on the Next 33 Years* (Macmillan, 1967). Introduces the concept of scenarios.

Zwicky, F., 'Morphological Astronomy', *The Observatory* 68:845 (August 1948), pp.121-143.

Richey, T., 'Problem Solving using Computer-Aided Morphological Analysis', *Journal of the Operational Research Society* 57 (2006), pp. 792-801.

Wilson, Jim, 'Skunk Works Magic', *Popular Mechanics* (September 1999), pp. 60-63.

Haynes, Leland, 'Clarence L. "Kelly" Johnson (1910-1990): Lockheed Aviation Legend – A Biography', SR-71 Blackbirds, WVI (June 2000).

Tolly, Kevin, 'The IBM PC Father: Remembering Don Estridge', *Network World* (20 December 2004).

Casnocha, Ben, 'Success on the Side', *The American* (24 April 2009). Bootlegging and 3M's experiences.

Sarasvathy, S.D. and Kotha, S., 'Dealing with Knightian uncertainty in the new economy: The Real Networks case' in J. Butler (ed.), *Research on Management and Entrepreneurship* 1 (Greenwich, CT, IAP Inc., 2001), pp. 31-62.

Sarasvathy, Saras, 'What Makes Entrepreneurs Entrepreneurial?', Darden Case Collection (Darden Business Publishing, University of Virginia, 2001).

Smit, Han T. J. and Trigeorgis, Lenos, *Strategic Investment: Real Options and Games* (Princeton University Press, 2004), pp. 176.

Klarreich, Erica, 'The Bidding Game', Beyond Discovery series, National Academy of Sciences (March 2003).

Binmore, Ken and Klemperer, Paul, 'The Biggest Auction Ever: the Sale of the British 3G Telecom Licences' (September 2001).

Chapter 6: Incubation – From Invention to Innovation

Hiltzik, Michael A., *Dealers of Lightning: Xerox PARC and the Dawn of the Computer Age* (Harper Paperbacks, 2000). A blog that reviews Hiltzik's book is Bunning, R., 'Reading Dealers of Lightning', Cincom Smalltalk (6 January 2006).

Glover, Julian and Milmo, Dan, 'Tracks of Our Tears – but now a new vision for trains is arriving', *Guardian* (5 August 2009).

Straw, Will, 'Global Innovation, British Innovation Policy: Lessons for the United States', *Science Progress* (12 January 2009).

Kao, John, *Innovation Nation: How America Is Losing Its Innovation Edge, Why It Matters, and What We Can Do to Get It Back* (Free Press, 2007).

Boyd, Drew, 'Innovation Dream Team', **www.innovationinpractice.com** (1 March 2009).

Naughton, John, 'Just as in Sinclair's day, Silicon Fen remains challenging ground', *Observer* (Sunday 11 October 2009).

Chapter 7: Future Imperfect

Voting Systems: The Jenkins Report, Research Paper 98/112 (10 December 1998).

Moyle, J.B. (trans.), *The Institutes of Justinian* (Clarendon Press, 5th edition, 1913). Title I, Book II, Section 1. For comments on the elements that by natural law are common to all.

Hardin, Garrett, 'The Tragedy of the Commons', *Science* 162:3859 (13 December 1968), pp. 1243-1248.

Allan, Tony, ' "Virtual water": a long-term solution for water short Middle Eastern economies?', Water Issues Group, School of Oriental & African Studies, University of London.

Martin, James, *The Meaning of the 21st Century* (Eden Books Project, 2006), pp. 9-10. The best time to be alive.

Index

Established Practice stifles 44, 60

Kirton Adaptation-Innovation Inventory (KAI) 174, 175, 197

government and 75-7, 201

military and 121

productisation 165, 173

intellectual property 42, 85, 87-9, 95, 170, 178, 179, 201, 203

internet 25, 26, 103-5, 107, 110-12, 139, 152-3, 154-5

invention 17, 25, 18, 72, 95, 164-5 *see also* inventor(s)

British 83-5

definition 163

Edison's 90

people notice 13

Six Sigma and 134

versus innovation 163-4

war and 89-90

War of the Currents 78-9

inventor(s) 186

al-Haythan, Ibn 88-9

Baylis, Trevor 178-9

Benz, Karl and Bertha 101-102

character of 79-82

J

Japan 47, 133-4

K

KAI *see* Kirton Adaptation-Innovation Inventory

Kawakita, Jiro 137-8, 144

Keis, Mary 81

Kirton Adaptation-Innovation Inventory (KAI) 174, 175, 197

Knight, Frank 9

four types of information 9-10

Knightian uncertainty 153-4

L

Lockheed 146, 174, 199

M

McGilchrist, Iain 23-4

Machiavelli, Niccolo 91

management 23, 24, 152, 165

modern mantra 24

over-measurement posing as prudent 40

project 128, 176-7

X

Z